Marriage Enrichment

Making a Good Marriage Better

Serendipity House / P.O. Box 1012 / Littleton, CO 80160

TOLL FREE 1-800-525-9563 / www.serendipityhouse.com

00 01 02 03 04 / **FN series•CHG** / 7 6 5 4 3 2 1

PROJECT ENGINEER
Lyman Coleman
Mike Shepherd

WRITING TEAM
Richard Peace, William Cutler, Andrew Sloan, Cathy Tardif

CARTOONS
Robert Schull

PRODUCTION TEAM
Christopher Werner, Sharon Penington, Erika Tiepel
The Serendipity Staff

ACKNOWLEDGMENTS

To Zondervan Bible Publishers
for permission to use
the NIV text, and Bible study notes
The Holy Bible, New International Bible Society.

Questions and Answers

1. **What is unique about this course?** The combination of three activities in one integrated program:
   - ❐ Learning about the issue
   - ❐ Interacting in Small Groups
   - ❐ Studying the Bible

2. **Who is it for?**
   - ❐ Home Bible Study groups
   - ❐ Sunday school and other church groups
   - ❐ Community organizations

3. **Where and how can I use this program?**
   - ❐ Classrooms with movable chairs
   - ❐ One-day seminars
   - ❐ Weekend retreats
   - ❐ Courses from seven to thirteen weeks

4. **How long is each session?** 90 minutes

5. **What if I do not have 90 minutes?** Divide sessions 1-6 into two sessions, making the course thirteen weeks instead of seven.

6. **How much does the course leader have to know about the subject?** Very little. This book provides all of the material. The leader convenes the meeting, makes introductory remarks, and follows the agenda.

7. **What about the group interaction?** This is directed by a Handout which each person is given at the beginning of the session. The Handout needs to be photocopied for every member. Another option is to provide each group member with his or her own course book (see page 5 for a detailed agenda to follow for each session.)

8. **Why do you divide into subgroups of 4 to 6?** To allow everyone to share.

9. **How would you go about dividing the group?** Divide the number of participants in the group by 4 to 6 to determine the number of subgroups needed. Then, ask the group to count off—1, 2, 3, etc.

10. **Would you have the same groups meet every session?** That is up to you. There are advantages both ways.

11. **How does this course fit into the larger educational structures of the church?** This is an entry level, short-term group for people with special needs or specific interests.

12. **Can this group continue as an ongoing small group after this course is over?** Yes. In the last session, the group is encouraged to make a contract or covenant for another 7 to 13 weeks, and move on to deeper Group Bible Study. A full description of the ongoing 201 Study courses are described inside the back cover.

13. **Are there other felt need courses available?** Yes, see page 61 for a complete list. For other curriculum for small groups, please call Serendipity at 1-800-525-9563.

CHECKLIST BEFORE THE SESSION

❒ ROOM ARRANGEMENT: Movable chairs for subdividing into groups of 4 to 6.

❒ HANDOUTS: Every person needs a Handout or the course book for every session. Permission is given for you to photocopy the Handout. Remember, there are two sides to the Handout. You may also want to photocopy the Caring Time part of the session as well.

❒ SPLIT SESSIONS: If you want to divide a session because you do not have 90 minutes, there is an ice-breaker to kick off the second part which you will need to photocopy from this book and give to the group.

❒ BIBLES: The Bible passage for discussion has been included in the Handout. However, if you want the group to read from their own Bibles, ask the people in the group to bring their Bibles.

❒ COURSE BOOK: Be sure to bring the book to the session and follow the agenda for each part of the session.

Agenda for Each Session

15 Minutes

ICE-BREAKER / Groups of 4 to 6
Divide the group into subgroups of 4 to 6 for a few minutes to get acquainted. Give the Handout—Side One to everyone.

You have permission to photocopy the Handout (both sides) for the session as needed, or you may prefer to provide each group member with his or her own course book.

5 Minutes

INTRODUCTION TO THE ISSUE / All Together
Bring the subgroups back together to listen to the introductory remarks for the session.

20 Minutes

DISCUSS THE ISSUE / Groups of 4 to 6
Regather in groups of 4 to 6 (same groups) to answer the questions on the Handout (Side One).

20 Minutes

BIBLE STUDY / Same Groups of 4 to 6
Stay in the same subgroups of 4 to 6 to discuss the Bible Study questions found on Side Two of the Handout.

Option 1: If you have a full 90 minutes for a session, follow the three-part agenda.

Option 2: If you only have 60 minutes for the session, do the Bible Study at the next session. A separate ice-breaker is provided for this Bible Study—which you will need to photocopy for group members.

20-30 Minutes

CARING TIME / Same Groups of 4 to 6
This is the most important part of every meeting. It is a time for sharing prayer requests and praying for one another. Be sure to stay with the agenda so that the Caring Time is not neglected.

SESSION
1

Setting Up House

OBJECTIVES

To help us get to know one another by sharing some pictures from our marriage memory book.

To consider the process of setting up a new home.

To reflect on how far we have come as couples.

To examine how one couple in the Bible began their life together.

THREE-PART AGENDA

ICE-BREAKER	ISSUE / BIBLE STUDY	CARING TIME
15 Minutes	45 Minutes	30 Minutes

OPTION: If you only have 60 minutes, divide this session into two sessions, with the Bible Study section for your next time together.

ICE-BREAKER

Pass out the Handout for this session or the course book to each person. Divide the group into subgroups of 4 to 6 to get acquainted by doing the Ice-Breaker. (Photocopy pages 9 and 11 as needed.)

1. When were you married? Where? How many attended?

2. What words best describe your wedding day?

❒ fun	❒ exciting	❒ tense	❒ a celebration
❒ sacred	❒ terrifying	❒ expensive	❒ dramatic
❒ a blur	❒ mystical	❒ hectic	❒ other:__________

3. What last minute advice did you receive from your family or friends before you got married?

4. What "memorable first" can you recall from setting up your home together? Your first joint purchase? Your first dinner guests? The first tradition you established? The first holiday on your own?

INTRODUCTION TO THE ISSUE

LEADER:

• Summarize these remarks (in your own words) into a brief introduction (no longer than 5 minutes).

• Be careful not to read the entire presentation to the group.

• In your presentation cover the "Discuss the Issue" questions listed on Side One of the Handout.

Getting married was great: all the excitement, the beauty of the service, the way family and friends rallied around with good cheer (and bad advice), all the presents. Then there was the honeymoon: small island, warm nights, lazy days, exotic sights and sounds (not that you noticed any of this very much). Moving into the apartment was a blast too: the chaos, boxes, collapsing chair, painting, erratic refrigerator.

But now you are settled. Your marriage has been successfully launched. So what is next? How do you get on with the task of developing a relationship? How does one lay a solid foundation for a relationship that is supposed to last a lifetime?

The late Walter Trobisch, a Christian marriage counselor and author, identified three essential steps in the process of moving from singleness to marriage: leaving, cleaving and becoming one flesh.[1] He bases this on the King James Version of Genesis 2:24 which states, "Therefore shall a man leave his father and his mother, and shall cleave unto his wife: and they shall be one flesh." Each step is important, each step has its own difficulties.

Leaving—The Act of Saying Good-bye

For Sandy and Jim, the act of saying good-bye to Sandy's parents was a long, drawn-out process, due largely to the fact that no one was sharing openly what they were feeling. Sandy's parents were afraid that their daughter didn't know what she was in for financially when she married Jim. Wanting to ease the shock for her without offending Jim, they decided to provide a regular allowance for Sandy.

Jim was not excited about the idea, but didn't say anything at first, lest he come across as ungrateful in response to his in-laws' generosity. Sandy, too, was afraid to bring up the subject during the first year of their marriage. She wanted to please her parents, and the extra spending money was helpful. On the other hand, she could see that Jim's frustration was growing (and his self-esteem was diminishing) with each parental gift.

The log jam of leaving finally broke for this couple when Sandy let Jim know she believed they could make it on their own, and she didn't want to receive her allowance any more. They announced the decision to Sandy's parents over a candlelight meal at Jim and Sandy's apartment. "Thanks for all you've done. We've appreciated the care you've shown. And now we are ready to take the financial responsibility on our own shoulders."

Walter Trobisch says, "There can be no marriage without leaving. Leaving is the price of happiness."[2] It is this act which permanently changes a man and woman's relationship with each other, with their parents and families, and with the community in general. When two people leave their father and mother in order to marry, they are signaling that a shift of responsibility is taking place from one generation to the next. This "leaving to being something new" provides the basis of security and partnership between spouses and forms the foundation of healthy relationships with parents and in-laws.

Cleaving—The Act of Making a Covenant

A second act essential to the beginning of marriage is cleaving. At first this seems too obvious to mention. "Of course we want to be together! Of course we're committed to each other! We're married, aren't we?" When couples "settle in" however, and ask themselves why they want to be together (or what they are committed to as a married couple), the issue tends to lose its clarity.

"I'm having trouble remaining committed to this relationship," reported Jeanne. "It turns out that Ken doesn't know where he's going, much less how to get there, and this is very troubling to me." Ken's perspective was quite different. "I can't figure Jeanne out. She's becoming so critical and impatient with me that I'm finding it hard to move forward in terms of my career or anything."

As the two of them shared their story, it became clear that the "glue" of their marriage wasn't holding. They needed help in translating their marriage vows into a unifying covenant between them. In Ken and Jeanne's case, the establishment of a plan to investigate seriously the three vocational options that interested Ken (coupled with his agreement to communicate regularly with Jeanne about "our future direction") got them moving in the right direction.

Becoming One Flesh—The Act of Celebrating

Becoming one flesh is that celebration which belongs to two people who have left their past behind and who have committed themselves to share everything in common as a faithful husband and wife. To "become one flesh," contrary to popular opinion (not to mention television and movies), is something which must be learned in order to be fully enjoyed.

The sexual part of marriage was, at first, very disappointing for Roger and Beth. Sexual experience had been so devalued in Beth's family that she assumed it was little more than a duty to be tolerated. Roger's understanding of sexual relationships came from a group of friends who had made sex the center of their lives. While he didn't fully accept their approach—he had a different attitude and different expectations—their views still influenced him. Roger was, in fact, a bit fearful that he would not be an adequate sexual partner. The fact that the celebration of their sexual life took some time in coming for Roger and Beth is not surprising.

The crucial thing is to open oneself fully to the process of becoming loving, sexual partners. This includes learning to appreciate the emotional, physical and spiritual side of sexuality. By learning to share thoughts and dreams, hopes and fears, successes and failures, material possessions as well as our bodies, we enter into the celebration of marriage. "By becoming one flesh," as Walter Trobisch puts it, "two whole persons become completely one, yet remain two different persons."[3]

Setting Up House

ICE-BREAKER / Groups of 4 to 6 / 15 Minutes

1. When were you married? Where? How many attended?
2. What words best describe your wedding day?
   ❒ fun ❒ exciting ❒ tense ❒ a celebration
   ❒ sacred ❒ terrifying ❒ expensive ❒ dramatic
   ❒ a blur ❒ mystical ❒ hectic ❒ other:________
3. What last minute advice did you receive from your family or friends before you got married?
4. What "memorable first" can you recall from setting up your home together? Your first joint purchase? Your first dinner guests? The first tradition you established? The first holiday on your own?

DISCUSS THE ISSUE / Same Groups / 20 Minutes

After a brief introduction by the leader, take turns sharing your responses to the following questions.

1. Some marriage counselors say "leaving" is the hardest part of establishing a good marriage in our society. What do you think makes "leaving" so hard?
   ❒ Parents have difficulty in letting go.
   ❒ Newlyweds fear taking responsibility for their lives.
   ❒ Newlyweds bring "unfinished business" or "leftovers" from a prior relationship.
   ❒ Newlyweds fear the financial realities in our economy.
   ❒ One partner is still tied emotionally to his or her parents.
2. When you were first married, how did you handle the task of establishing yourselves as a married couple in relation to the following?
   • your parents • your in-laws • your old roommates
   • your siblings • other relatives • your friends
3. On the scale below, how would you rate your progress at becoming comfortable with your identity as a married pair?

   We've only just begun ______________________________ **Everything's coming up roses**
4. What do you think is the most common difficulty newly married couples face when it comes to developing a satisfying sexual life?
   ❒ lack of knowledge ❒ too much knowledge
   ❒ unrealistic expectations ❒ false expectations
   ❒ a harmful sexual history ❒ puritanical view of sex
   ❒ the differing needs and expectations of men and women

INTRODUCTION TO THE BIBLE STUDY

Despite its many forms and various expressions, marriage remains one of the great constants in human history. According to the Bible, the institution of marriage was established at the time of creation. In other words, it is part of God's creative purpose. It is the one relationship, lifted above all others, meant to fulfill the primary needs a man and a woman have for each other. So central and so sacred is marriage that it is used in the New Testament as the analogy that most fully represents the relationship which Christ has established with his people, the church.

All of this lends hope that marriages may be formed which will not only survive, but thrive. The starting point for such confidence is the familiar story of Adam and Eve in the Garden of Eden. Take another look at the text and see how this couple "set up house."

ICE-BREAKER FOR TWO-SESSION OPTION

If you are doing the Bible Study as a separate session, start off this session by dividing this group into subgroups of 4 to 6 and answering the following questions. Photocopy and give this to the group.

Your Needs, My Needs. When we get married, we all bring a set of needs which we expect will be met by our spouses. Different people have different expectations. Men and women have different expectations. So it is important to be aware of our needs and those of our spouse. Answer both of these questions on your own. Then each person can share their answers with the group.

1. Listed below are 10 common needs which people expect marriage to fulfill. Rank the top five needs in order of importance to you (1 = most important):

_____ admiration / respect
_____ affection
_____ attractive spouse
_____ domestic support
_____ family commitment
_____ financial security
_____ honesty and trust
_____ open communication
_____ recreational companionship
_____ sexual fulfillment

2. Now rank the top five needs you think your spouse has chosen:

_____ admiration / respect
_____ affection
_____ attractive spouse
_____ domestic support
_____ family commitment
_____ financial security
_____ honesty and trust
_____ open communication
_____ recreational companionship
_____ sexual fulfillment

SESSION ONE BIBLE STUDY

15 The LORD God took the man and put him in the Garden of Eden to work it and
take care of it. 16 And the LORD God commanded the man, "You are free to eat from
any tree in the garden; 17 but you must not eat from the tree of knowledge of good and evil,
for when you eat of it you will surely die."

18 The LORD God said, "It is not good for the man to be alone. I will make a helper suitable for him."

19 Now the LORD God had formed out of the ground all the beasts of the field and all the
birds of the air. He brought them to the man to see what he would name them; and whatever the man called each living creature, that was its name. 20 So the man gave names to
all the livestock, the birds of the air and all the beasts of the field.

But for Adam no suitable helper was found. 21 So the LORD God caused the man to fall
into a deep sleep; and while he was sleeping, he took one of the man's ribs and closed up
the place with flesh. 22 Then the LORD God made a woman from the rib he had taken out of
the man, and he brought her to the man.

23 The man said,

> *"This is now bone of my bones*
> *and flesh of my flesh;*
> *she shall be called 'woman,'*
> *for she was taken out of man."*

24 For this reason a man will leave his father and mother and be united to his wife, and they will become one flesh.

25 The man and his wife were both naked, and they felt no shame.

Genesis 2:15–25

1. Why do you think God said it was not good for Adam to be alone?

2. What did God mean when he described woman as a "helper"?

3. When Adam saw Eve, he felt an instant kinship with her ("bone of my bones and flesh of my flesh"). When you first became acquainted with your spouse, what did you see in him or her that made you feel that same kinship?

4. In the Garden of Eden, Adam and Eve experienced a time of idyllic, wide-eyed innocence. What is the closest you've come to such a time in your relationship and time together as a couple?

- ❐ when we were first dating
- ❐ the day we fell in love
- ❐ our first year of marriage
- ❐ We're still experiencing it.
- ❐ other:____________________

REFERENCE NOTES

Genesis 2:15–25

2:18 ***not good ... to be alone.*** God knows our need for companionship. The human race also depends on partners to procreate and multiply, to thus "fill the earth and subdue it" (1:28; 2:19–20). It could also be that two—male and female—reflect God's image better than one alone. This does not imply, however, that single people are an incomplete image of God.

helper suitable for him. This does not imply docile subservience for the woman—rather, she is an active sustainer and source of strength—as God himself is often described as "helper" (see Ps. 10:14; 30:10; 54:4; 115:9–11; Hos. 13:9).

2:20 ***Adam.*** Adam means "the man," also "of earth," in Hebrew. In 3:20, Adam names his wife Eve. Eve probably means "living" or "life-giving."

2:22 ***God made a woman from the rib ... of the man.*** This begs, but does not answer, the proverbial question. "Which came first—the chicken or the egg?" The first woman evidently came from the man, but thereafter, all men are borne by women. Thus both are interdependent—on each other and on God. Being made of Adam's rib signifies that woman is part of man, and together they are of the same flesh and bones, even "one flesh" (2:23–24).

2:24 ***leave his father and mother.*** For a man to take a wife and form a new family unit, he must break free of his parents' protection and custody. Likewise for a woman. This has physical, psychological and financial implications for all parties.

be united. This is the act of "cleaving" or "bonding," as with glue. This has come to imply making a public commitment or stipulating a long-term covenant.

become one flesh. By the act of physical union and sexual intimacy, something synergistic and spiritual has happened, such that the total effect is greater than the sum of the parts. "They are no longer two, but one" (see Matthew 19:3–6).

2:25 ***naked ... no shame.*** This signifies moral innocence, which would soon be lost as a result of the Fall (3:7). Ever since, men and women are prone to cover up their shame.

CARING TIME

Take time now to share any personal prayer requests. Start out by asking everyone to answer the question:

"How can we help you in prayer this week?"

Take turns praying for each other, remembering the requests that have been shared. If you would like to pray in silence, say the word "Amen" when you have finished your prayer, so that the next person will know when to start. At the close, join hands and pray this prayer together:

"Dear God, Thank you for the gift of my spouse.
Help us to always make you the center of our marriage,
and to be united in glorifying you.
Thank you also for bringing this group together.
Help us to become a supportive, loving and
caring group that can build up each
marriage represented here. Amen."

LEADER:

If applicable, have the group use the extra space on this page for group prayer requests.

SESSION

2

Respectfully Yours

OBJECTIVES

To identify the expectations we bring into marriage.

To consider the adjustments we are called to make after we get married.

To learn how to say to each other, "I remain respectfully yours."

To explore the issue of mutual respect in the Bible.

THREE-PART AGENDA

ICE-BREAKER	ISSUE / BIBLE STUDY	CARING TIME
15 Minutes	45 Minutes	30 Minutes

OPTION: If you only have 60 minutes, divide this session into two sessions, with the Bible Study section for your next time together.

ICE-BREAKER

Pass out the Handout for this session or the course book to each person. Divide the group into subgroups of 4 to 6 to get acquainted by doing the Ice-Breaker. (Photocopy pages 17 and 19 as needed.)

1. Before you were married, what were the top five traits you wanted in a mate?

❐ good-looking
❐ slim
❐ great figure
❐ sensitive
❐ loves kids
❐ sense of humor
❐ romantic
❐ generous
❐ tall
❐ nonsmoker
❐ sophisticated
❐ sincere
❐ stable
❐ well-educated
❐ intelligent
❐ gentle
❐ enjoys travel
❐ spontaneous
❐ mature
❐ spiritual
❐ caring
❐ athletic
❐ dependable
❐ other:__________

2. Where do you think these expectations come from?

❐ parental role model (a girl just like Mom, a boy just like Dad)
❐ peer influence
❐ church's teaching
❐ TV values
❐ personal reflection

INTRODUCTION TO THE ISSUE

LEADER:

- **Summarize these remarks (in your own words) into a brief introduction (no longer than 5 minutes).**
- **Be careful not to read the entire presentation to the group.**
- **In your presentation cover the "Discuss the Issue" questions listed on Side One of the Handout.**

The young couple was in Pastor Benson's office within a year after their wedding date. Unhappiness was written all over their faces. "We wanted to talk to you right away since it seems we are getting off on the wrong foot in our marriage," said Andy. Liz silently nodded agreement. With a little encouragement, they began to tell their story. What unfolded was a description of frustrations based on differing expectations of what marriage would be like. Liz was surprised by some of Andy's behaviors which he considered "normal." For example, there was his habit of turning the stereo on full blast whenever he entered the room. "How can I talk to Andy with all that noise blasting through his speakers?" she complained. Andy's reaction was to label Liz's expectations as "unrealistic." "We just don't have to talk all the time," he said.

Walter Wangerin identifies three phases of adjustment in relationships: idealization, realization and mutualization. In the idealization phase, people tend to falsify the information about their partners. This is not done maliciously, but as a means of persuading ourselves that it is okay to marry this person who has come into our lives. Walter Wangerin expresses it this way:

> Love lies a little. Love, the desire to like and be liked, feels so good when it is satisfied, that it never wants to stop. Therefore love edits the facts in order to continue to feel good. Love allows me an innocent misperception of my fiancée, while it encourages in her a favorable misperception of myself. If it isn't blind, it does squint a bit. Love idealizes both of us.[4]

For example, if I love a rigorous climb in the mountains, I idealize the joy my spouse will have pursuing the same summit. Then comes the realization phase, in which I discover who my spouse really is, what she is capable of doing, and what she likes to do. It turns out that my spouse doesn't like rigorous mountain climbs. Romantic walks on the seashore have always been her preference. Some call this phase the "Disappointment Phase" or "end of the honeymoon." By whatever name, we all know it as the process of adjustment which every couple inevitably must go through.

At the core of our disappointment is the sense that our new mate does not live up to our expectations. But where do these expectations come from? Since no two people will draw their expectations from identical sources (parents, communities, churches, favorite television personalities, books, friends, etc.), we must first figure out what the frame of reference is for each partner. While some insight may be gained during courtship, the majority of our discoveries occur after we marry, for only then are we in a real, permanent relationship (where such different expectations begin to matter).

But discovering the sources of our differing expectations is not the end of this early marriage work. Once you realize that you have differing expectations, what do you do? How do you adjust? There are at least three strategies people have used.

Three Ways to Adjust Your Unrealistic Expectations

1. **The Hierarchical Model.** This way of adjustment proposes to solve the problem of differing expectations by placing one person in charge, and putting the other person in the role of submission to this authority. Bill and Cindy established this approach in their marriage. When Bill was invited by his employer to consider an overseas assignment (which would take him away from his wife for three months), he carefully consulted several counselors and then prepared to announce his decision to his wife. Meanwhile, Cindy prayed about his decision, and especially about her willingness to accept whatever Bill determined was best. Fortunately, Bill was a gentleman who esteemed his wife and considered her his equal. This greatly helped Cindy accept her role of responder to Bill's role of initiator.
2. **The Negotiation Model.** This way of adjustment proposes to solve the expectations/adjustment dilemma by making deals. This worked well for Ellen and Harry, who sought to come to consensus about career, household responsibilities and leisure time pursuits. They began with the area where there was the most agreement: how to spend their free weekends. Since both were avid hikers (this is how they met in the first place), the only issue was when and where to go camping. When it came to the issue of careers and household responsibility, however, Harry had always expected that his wife would stay home and raise a family, while Ellen was eager to get on with her career as an artist. This issue took a lot of discussion in order to come up with ways both could feel fulfilled and both could be happy about how the family ran. This approach takes time since no one is "in charge." But in the end it brings great stability, since everything is out in the open and no one is forced to accept a role that is uncomfortable to him or her.
3. **The Mutualization Model.** This way of adjustment proposes to solve the expectations/adjustment problem by determining what's best for the relationship. This differs from the open negotiation model, since in this case the focus is on the relationship and not on the individuals. The emphasis has shifted from "my rights" to "our relationship." That's what Mark and Jean committed themselves to when they lit the unity candle at their wedding. They decided that their relationship was more important than either one's personal promotion at work. This decision helped them determine how they spent their leisure time, how they responded to overtime requests at the office, and how they would face new career opportunities. So far, the marriage is still going strong, based on the Mutualization strategy: "To let the concerns of the relationship take precedence over their concern for their individual lives."[5]

SESSION TWO HANDOUT: Marriage Enrichment

Respectfully Yours

ICE-BREAKER / Groups of 4 to 6 / 15 Minutes

1. Before you were married, what were the top five traits you wanted in a mate?

❒ good-looking ❒ tall ❒ enjoys travel ❒ slim
❒ nonsmoker ❒ spontaneous ❒ great figure ❒ sophisticated
❒ mature ❒ sensitive ❒ sincere ❒ spiritual
❒ loves kids ❒ stable ❒ caring ❒ sense of humor
❒ well-educated ❒ athletic ❒ romantic ❒ intelligent
❒ dependable ❒ generous ❒ gentle ❒ other:__________

2. Where do you think these expectations come from?

❒ peer influence ❒ church's teaching
❒ TV values ❒ personal reflection
❒ parental role model (a girl just like Mom, a boy just like Dad)

DISCUSS THE ISSUE / Same Groups / 20 Minutes

After a brief introduction by the leader, take turns sharing your responses to the following questions.

1. Where would you place yourself on the Idealization-Realization continuum below (circle one of the numbers)?

1	2	3	4	5
Above the clouds! No problems.	**Turbulence aloft! We have a difference of opinion.**	**Descending rapidly! What strange expectations.**	**Fasten seat belts! Let's face facts.**	**Feet on the ground! I accept you as you are.**

2. Which of these models typifies the way you adjust your differing expectations?

❒ Hierarchical Model—one person in charge.
❒ Negotiation Model—we reach consensus.
❒ Mutualization Model—we both work to find what's best for the relationship.

3. In building your own strategy for dealing with expectations and adjustments, what will you include in your plan (choose two or three most important to you)?

❒ clear spelling out of roles
❒ open discussion of needs and desires
❒ lots of serendipity (surprise discoveries)
❒ recognition of how the past impacts on our present
❒ enough space to grow and change
❒ agreement to put the relationship ahead of our individual desires

INTRODUCTION TO THE BIBLE STUDY

In *Webster's New Collegiate Dictionary,* we read these definitions of submit: "to yield oneself to the authority or will of another; to defer to the opinion or authority of another; to commit to another; to make available." The meaning of these definitions is easy enough to grasp. It is when they are applied that all the difficulties arise.

Traditionally, it is the woman who feels the impact of submission first. Thus, it is she who asks the question first: "Do you mean to tell me I have to submit to him?" There's actually another starting point. When Paul discusses the relationship between husband and wife, he begins by calling for mutual submission (Eph. 5:21). Then in discussing this concept, he offers a series of practical suggestions for how marriages work.

ICE-BREAKER FOR TWO-SESSION OPTION

If you are doing the Bible Study as a separate session, start off this session by dividing this group into subgroups of 4 to 6 and answering the following questions. Photocopy and give this to the group.

Think back to your parent's marriage and the different roles they took on and modeled for you. Look over the roles defined below and decide which ones were typically fulfilled in your family by the husband (indicate with an "H"), which ones were typically fulfilled in your family by the wife (indicate with a "W"), and which ones were fulfilled in your family by both spouses (indicate with a "B").

_____ took out the garbage
_____ did most of the "babysitting"
_____ paid for family meals out
_____ made the meals at home
_____ drove the family to church
_____ earned most of the money
_____ spent most of the money
_____ packed the suitcase for trips
_____ did more of the inside housework
_____ took more leisure and recreation time
_____ did more of the outside housework
_____ coached kids with homework, chores
_____ hired the babysitter
_____ drove the kids to school
_____ balanced the checkbook
_____ set the budget priorities
_____ was home for lunch
_____ packed car for trips

Look over this list one more time and indicate for your present relationship which of these roles and duties you view as "Man's work" (= "M"), which you view as "Woman's work" (= "F"), and which is "Negotiable" or "Neither" (= "N").

SESSION TWO BIBLE STUDY

21 Submit to one another out of reverence for Christ.

22 Wives, submit to your husbands as to the Lord. 23 For the husband is the head of the wife as Christ is the head of the church, his body, of which he is the Savior. 24 Now as the church submits to Christ, so also wives should submit to their husbands in everything.

25 Husbands, love your wives, just as Christ loved the church and gave himself up for her 26 to make her holy, cleansing her by the washing with water through the word, 27 and to present her to himself as a radiant church, without stain or wrinkle or any other blemish, but holy and blameless. 28 In this same way, husbands ought to love their wives as their own bodies. He who loves his wife loves himself. 29 After all, no one ever hated his own body, but he feeds and cares for it, just as Christ does the church—30 for we are members of his body. 31 "For this reason a man will leave his father and mother and be united to his wife, and the two will become one flesh." 32 This is a profound mystery—but I am talking about Christ and the church. 33 However, each one of you also must love his wife as he loves himself, and the wife must respect her husband.

Ephesians 5:21–33

1. What does it mean for a husband to love his wife in the way Paul describes here? What does it mean for a wife to respect her husband?

2. What does the concept of mutual submission suggest to you?
❒ Both partners are equal.
❒ It will never work.
❒ Domination is not what marriage is all about.
❒ There is no "boss" in the family.
❒ Marriage makes demands on both partners to make it work.
❒ Men are called upon to give up their traditional leadership role.
❒ Compromises rather than demands are required.

3. Who do you look to as a role model for a good marriage?

4. Who do you turn to for advice in your marriage?
❒ parents or other family members
❒ another couple
❒ a counselor / pastor
❒ a business associate
❒ a completely unexpected person

5. When is it toughest to support your marriage partner?

6. Where is God in the nitty-gritty details of your relationship right now?
❒ He is putting us through some tough tests right now.
❒ He is mysteriously absent as far as anyone can tell.
❒ He is the strength in our weakness.
❒ He is causing us to esteem each other more highly.

REFERENCE NOTES

Ephesians 5:21–33

5:21 ***Submit to one another.*** The concept of mutual submission is key to understanding the relationship between husband and wife. In the verses that follow, Paul will explain what this means for the wife (vv. 22–24) and for the husband (vv. 25–33).

5:22 ***Wives.*** In a radical departure from tradition, Paul addresses women in their own right as individuals, able to make their own choices. He does not address them through their husbands (as was common in the first century). He does not tell husbands: "Make your wives submit to you." He speaks to wives on the same level as he will speak next to husbands.

submit. This injunction from Paul must be understood in its historical context. In Jewish law, a woman was a "thing," not a person, and she had no legal rights. In describing the Greek world, Demosthenes, wrote, "We have courtesans for our pleasure, prostitutes for daily physical use, wives to bring up legitimate children." In Rome, too, divorce was easy, and women were repressed. Against this, Paul proposes a radical, liberating view: (1) submission was to be mutual (the man was no longer the absolute authority); (2) wives are called upon to defer only to their husbands (and not to every man); and (3) submission is defined and qualified by Christ's headship of the church (Christ died for the church).

5:23 ***Christ is the head of the church.*** The word "head" when used today has the sense of "ruler" or "authority." In Greek, when "head" is used in a metaphorical sense as it is here, it means "origin," as in the "source (head) of a river." Woman has her origins in man (see Gen. 2:18–23), just as the church has its origin in Christ. Had Paul wanted to convey the idea that the husband "rules over" the wife (as Christ "rules over" the church), he would have used a different Greek word for "head."

the Savior. The emphasis in this analogy is not on Christ as Lord, but on Christ as Savior. Paul is not saying that husbands are to express "headship" via the exertion of some sort of authority (as befits a "lord"), but via the expression of sacrificial love as characterized by the Savior.

5:25 ***love your wives.*** This is the main thing Paul says to husbands. It is so important that he repeats this injunction three times (vv. 25,28,33). Love is what the husband gives by way of his part in the mutual submission paradigm. This attitude stands in contrast to Jewish teaching. "The rabbis asserted that money, the contract, and intercourse make marriage. When they enumerated what else a man 'owed' to his wife, they seldom mentioned love" (Barth).

just as Christ loved the church and gave himself up for her. Paul makes quite clear in what sense he is speaking of Christ as head over the church. Two actions characterize Christ's role for the church: love and sacrifice. The husband is called to act toward his wife in the same way—that is, to die for her! (This is how Christ "gave himself up for the church.") A wife is asked to "submit" not to "authority," but to "sacrifical love."

CARING TIME

Remember that this time is for developing and expressing your caring for each other as group members. You can do this by sharing any personal prayer requests and praying for each other's needs. Start by answering the question:

"How do you need God's help in loving and respecting your spouse?"

Then share any personal prayer requests and take turns praying for each other. Close by taking a few minutes for each group member to say a brief prayer of thanks for one or two characteristics and strengths that he or she respects in their spouse.

LEADER:

If applicable, have the group use the extra space on this page for group prayer requests.

SESSION

3

We Can Work It Out

OBJECTIVES

To become better acquainted with the issue of conflict in marriage.

To consider various responses that couples make when faced with conflict in their relationship.

To gain encouragement from the Bible that when it comes to conflict, "We can work it out."

THREE-PART AGENDA

ICE-BREAKER	ISSUE / BIBLE STUDY	CARING TIME
15 Minutes	45 Minutes	30 Minutes

OPTION: If you only have 60 minutes, divide this session into two sessions, with the Bible Study section for your next time together.

ICE-BREAKER

Pass out the Handout for this session or the course book to each person. Divide the group into subgroups of 4 to 6 to do the Ice-Breaker. (Photocopy pages 25 and 27 as needed.)

Take a vote on each statement below. Do you agree or disagree?

	Agree	Disagree
The couple that fights together stays together.	❒	❒
The sooner a couple addresses a problem, the better.	❒	❒
Conflict is always wrong.	❒	❒
Finding the "principle of the thing" is the key to resolving conflict.	❒	❒
Christian couples seldom fight.	❒	❒
In most conflicts, it is hardly ever black and white, right or wrong; therefore there is no winner or loser to identify.	❒	❒
The presence of conflict shows that you have an honest relationship.	❒	❒
Conflict breeds discontent in a marriage and drives people apart.	❒	❒
Direct confrontation is the only constructive way to face conflict.	❒	❒
Disagreement is not necessary if you have open communication.	❒	❒
Yielding one's rights is the best starting point for solving problems.	❒	❒
Sticking to one's rights is important for personal growth.	❒	❒
Great marriages are built on compromise.	❒	❒
Conflict is so basic to a relationship that it is impossible to have any closeness without it.	❒	❒
There is a difference between a good fight and a dirty fight, and the latter is to be avoided.	❒	❒

INTRODUCTION TO THE ISSUE

LEADER:

• Summarize these remarks (in your own words) into a brief introduction (no longer than 5 minutes).

• Be careful not to read the entire presentation to the group.

• In your presentation cover the "Discuss the Issue" questions listed on Side One of the Handout.

"Fight or Flight"—the alternatives present themselves quite early in the first year of marriage. A small irritation gets under the skin. It is hardly noticeable to the unaided eye. But to the feeling heart, the irritation takes a central place. Immediately a choice presents itself: Shall I fight this contradiction, this hurt, this cutting remark by my spouse? Or shall I withdraw?

To fight will most likely result in a victory or a defeat for each spouse. If I am sufficiently strong in my response, I may overcome my marriage partner's irritation. But what kind of victory will I gain? Will I be happy winning if it means that my partner loses? And what if my counterattack isn't powerful enough? Will the small irritation expand into a major quarrel, leaving a wound within my heart?

Ginny didn't like the prospect of fighting with her husband, Stan. She chose to withdraw whenever conflict threatened. She seldom withdrew physically, but she became an expert in yielding and in covering up the hurt and anger she felt. Stan was strangely unaware of Ginny's tactics—so much so that he frequently boasted to his friends that he knew this was a "marriage made in heaven," because they had no arguments.

Then one day it happened. Another irritation came from Stan. It was "no big deal" from his point of view, "an issue easily resolved." But Ginny couldn't handle it. She screamed, "I've had it. I'm sick and tired of your abuse. I quit!" and left the house.

Stan and Ginny's marriage may have been made in heaven, but it had to be lived on earth, where conflict is a part of life. Ginny's yielding may have preserved their relationship for a short time, but when it became an established pattern of response to conflict, it became counterproductive. Of course, it wasn't only Ginny who held an inadequate strategy for dealing with conflict. Stan's assumption that all was well (because there weren't any arguments) gave him away as one whose eyes were firmly fixed on himself alone.

Stan and Ginny both would have benefited from Walter Trobisch's famous "Six Tests of Love." "The fifth test is the Quarrel Test," writes Trobisch. "When a couple comes to me and wants to get married, I always ask them if they have once had a real quarrel—not just a casual difference of opinion, but a real fight. Many times they will say: 'Oh, no! Pastor, we love each other.' Then I tell them: 'Quarrel first—and then I will marry you.' The point is, of course, not the quarreling, but the ability to be reconciled to each other."[6]

Certainly not all fighting fulfills this positive purpose. Manipulative fighting or "winning-at-all-costs" fighting (in which one person controls the other's response) is not constructive. Neither is fighting which is insensitive to the other's emotional or mental state. Fighting which inflicts psychological or physical injury is destructive and can never be justified. Likewise, fighting which attacks another person's identity or significance as a person contributes nothing but harm.

Either partner who is tempted to bring such destructive elements into marital fights must heed the instructions once popularized in the Wild West: "Leave your weapons at the door!" There is no place in marriage for such approaches. The sooner couples lay down these weapons, the sooner they will begin to move toward resolving conflict.

The central issue in working out conflict, then, is not whether to have a fight, but how to have a good fight. Here are eight ground rules for having a good fight, suggested by counselor Angela Pintar. Perhaps you will want to add your own.

1. **Fight by mutual consent.** Don't insist on a fight at a time when one of you can't handle the strain. A good fight demands two ready partners.
2. **Stick to the present.** Don't dredge up past mistakes and faults about which you can do nothing.
3. **Stick to the subject.** Limit this fight to this subject. Don't throw every other problem into it; take them one at a time.
4. **Don't hit below the belt.** In your life together you discover each other's sensitive areas. Don't throw them at each other.
5. **Aim to resolve rather than to win.** Win/lose fights cause resentments to accumulate within a relationship.
6. **Don't quit; work it out.** Bring the fight to a mutual conclusion. Otherwise it will just recur again and again.
7. **Respect crying.** Crying is a valid response to how you feel and how the other feels. But don't let crying sidetrack you. Sometimes it is a signal for a time-out.
8. **No violence.** Physical violence violates all the above rules for fighting by mutual consent.[7]

Ginny didn't continue her flight forever. She was persuaded to identify and deal with the irritations she had stuffed away during her marriage. At first this new approach was almost as rough for Stan as Ginny's disappearance was. The "world according to Stan" was shaken and stretched by Ginny's decision to deal with the irritations she had experienced. But eventually Stan and Ginny cleared the hurdle of residual resentments and began to deal with their conflicts as they arose. Now, when it comes to conflicts, they stand in agreement with George Bach who declares: "The family that fights together stays together."[8]

We Can Work It Out

ICE-BREAKER / Groups of 4 to 6 / 15 Minutes

Take a vote on each statement below. Do you agree or disagree?

	Agree	Disagree
The couple that fights together stays together.	❐	❐
The sooner a couple addresses a problem, the better.	❐	❐
Conflict is always wrong.	❐	❐
Finding the "principle of the thing" is the key to resolving conflict.	❐	❐
Christian couples seldom fight.	❐	❐
In most conflicts, it is hardly ever black and white, right or wrong; therefore there is no winner or loser to identify.	❐	❐
The presence of conflict shows that you have an honest relationship.	❐	❐
Conflict breeds discontent in a marriage and drives people apart.	❐	❐
Direct confrontation is the only constructive way to face conflict.	❐	❐
Disagreement is not necessary if you have open communication.	❐	❐
Yielding one's rights is the best starting point for solving problems.	❐	❐
Sticking to one's rights is important for personal growth.	❐	❐
Great marriages are built on compromise.	❐	❐
Conflict is so basic to a relationship that it is impossible to have any closeness without it.	❐	❐
There is a difference between a good fight and a dirty fight, and the latter is to be avoided.	❐	❐

DISCUSS THE ISSUE / Same Groups / 20 Minutes

After a brief introduction by the leader, take turns sharing your responses to the following questions.

1. If Stan and Ginny had come to you for help in resolving their conflict, what would you have said?
   - ❐ "Give it time."
   - ❐ "Fight it out."
   - ❐ "I've got a good divorce lawyer to recommend."
   - ❐ "Be honest, but gentle."
   - ❐ "Don't worry; be happy."

2. When did you first realize that your "marriage made in heaven" had to be lived on earth—that is, in the midst of conflict?
   - ❐ before we were married
   - ❐ on the honeymoon
   - ❐ within the first month of marriage
   - ❐ just today
   - ❐ "What conflict?"

3. Which ground rules for a good fight have been most important in your marriage?
   - _____ fight by mutual consent
   - _____ stick to the present
   - _____ stick to the subject
   - _____ don't hit below the belt
   - _____ aim to resolve rather than to win
   - _____ don't quit; work it out
   - _____ respect crying
   - _____ no violence

INTRODUCTION TO THE BIBLE STUDY

From beginning to end in the Bible, you will find fighting. From Genesis to Revelation, we see people attack, blame, undermine, manipulate, take advantage of, get even with, run over and run away from each other. They do this with amazing skill. What we don't see (at least not very frequently) are people skilled in living together in right relationships. Not surprisingly, the New Testament is filled with advice about how to restore broken relationships. Such admonitions would not be necessary if relationships flowed easily and smoothly. All this should tell us something—namely, how nearly impossible it is for imperfect, sinful people to get along with each other. We need God's help to overcome our relational conflicts.

In Ephesians, the apostle Paul introduces us to life "in Christ." According to Paul, being in Christ lets us in on God's plan "to bring all things in heaven and earth together under one head, even Christ" (Eph. 1:10). Although we must wait for the perfect fulfillment of this promise, it is possible (not to mention desirable) to work toward such unity in the here-and-now in our ongoing relationships with others.

ICE-BREAKER FOR TWO-SESSION OPTION

If you are doing the Bible Study as a separate session, start off this session by dividing this group into subgroups of 4 to 6 and answering the following questions. Photocopy and give this to the group.

1. When you were young, what did you and other members of the family quarrel about the most?
   - ❒ getting the best seat in the car
   - ❒ getting the biggest piece of dessert
   - ❒ allowances
   - ❒ privileges and chores
   - ❒ choice of activities
   - ❒ choice of friends

2. In fight terms, how did you see yourself when you faced quarrels when you were first married?
   - ❒ going after another victory
   - ❒ trying to avoid another defeat
   - ❒ too vulnerable
   - ❒ too guarded
   - ❒ coming into fighting form
   - ❒ retired from the ring
   - ❒ ready to compromise
   - ❒ ready to throw in the towel
   - ❒ outclassed
   - ❒ equal to the challenge

SESSION THREE BIBLE STUDY

[17]So I tell you this, and insist on it in the Lord, that you must no longer live as the
Gentiles do, in the futility of their thinking. [18]They are darkened in their under-
standing and separated from the life of God because of the ignorance that is in them due
to the hardening of their hearts. [19]Having lost all sensitivity, they have given themselves
over to sensuality so as to indulge in every kind of impurity, with a continual lust for more.
[20]You, however, did not come to know Christ that way. [21]Surely you heard of him and
were taught in him in accordance with the truth that is in Jesus. [22]You were taught, with
regard to your former way of life, to put off your old self, which is being corrupted by its
deceitful desires; [23]to be made new in the attitude of your minds; [24]and to put on the new
self, created to be like God in true righteousness and holiness.
[25]Therefore each of you must put off falsehood and speak truthfully to his neighbor, for
we are all members of one body. [26]"In your anger do not sin": Do not let the sun go down
while you are still angry, [27]and do not give the devil a foothold. [28]He who has been stealing
must steal no longer, but must work, doing something useful with his own hands, that he
may have something to share with those in need.
[29]Do not let any unwholesome talk come out of your mouths, but only what is helpful
for building others up according to their needs, that it may benefit those who listen. [30]And
do not grieve the Holy Spirit of God, with whom you were sealed for the day of redemp-
tion. [31]Get rid of all bitterness, rage and anger, brawling and slander, along with every form
of malice. [32]Be kind and compassionate to one another, forgiving each other, just as in
Christ God forgave you.

Ephesians 4:17–32

1. What makes it possible to live as a "new person" the way Paul insists upon?

2. Why is truthful speech so important to right relationships?
❒ It changes strangers into friends.
❒ It is the basis of trust.
❒ Anything else tears people apart.
❒ It takes truthfulness to maintain meaningful relationships.

3. When you get angry with your spouse, what's the best way to keep from sinning?
❒ stuff it, keep the feelings inside
❒ settle it before sundown
❒ speak about it openly
❒ apologize if necessary
❒ don't let anger turn into resentment
❒ blame the devil for it
❒ try to differentiate between wounded pride and real wrong

4. Have each person finish this sentence, directing their answer to their spouse: "One way I have seen the 'new life' emerge in you is ..."
❒ in your understanding of what God is like
❒ in the way you speak to me
❒ in the way you handle anger and conflict
❒ in the way you forgive
❒ in the way you share with those in need
❒ other:____________
❒ in the way you work to build me up

REFERENCE NOTES

Ephesians 4:17–32

4:17 *as the Gentiles do.* Paul begins this section on purity of life by describing the typical Gentile lifestyle from which Christians must flee. Paul emphasizes the connection between thought and behavior. By means of three phrases, he hammers home his point that Gentiles live as they do because their thinking is amiss. He points to "the futility of their thinking," to the fact that "they are darkened in their understanding," and to their "ignorance." Right thinking does matter if a person is to get on with right living.

4:22–24 *put off your old self ... put on the new self.* This taking on a whole new way of thinking and acting is something that one does penitently at conversion, and continually as a Christian. This is a past action in which we have experienced a new creation, upon which a future command (v. 25) is predicated, that is, the renewal of the new mind we have been given (see parallel in Col. 3:9–10).

4:25 *put off falsehood and speak truthfully.* Because falsehood destroys community (which is built on trust), Christians are counted on to always speak truth and thus build up the fellowship.

4:26 *"In your anger, do not sin."* Paul recognizes that there is such a thing as legitimate anger. He says in 5:6 that God experiences anger, though the translation obscures this meaning. (Although the phrase in 5:6 is rendered as "God's wrath," the same word is used there which is here translated "anger.") Jesus was angry (Mark 3:5). There are certain situations in which anger is the only honest response. For Christians to deny their anger is dangerous and self-defeating. But once admitted, anger is to be dealt with, and so Paul identifies four ways to deal with anger. First, "in your anger do not sin." What is the source of the anger? Is it wounded pride or real wrong? Is it spite or is it injustice? In verse 31, Paul will point out that "unrighteous anger" is to be eliminated. Second, "do not let the sun go down" on your anger; that is, deal with it quickly. Do not nurse anger and let it grow. Third, do not let anger develop into resentment. This is what the word translated "angry" at the end of verse 26 means. Get the anger out in the open. Be reconciled if possible. Apologize if necessary. Fourth, "do not give the devil a foothold." Do not let Satan exploit your anger, turning it into hostility (or using it to disrupt fellowship).

4:29 *only what is helpful.* As in the restriction in verse 28 (where benevolence is to replace thievery), so here, edifying speech is to replace "unwholesome" (rotten, vulgar) talk.

4:30 *grieve the Holy Spirit.* By sins in word and deed, we offend this sensitive, holy person, who can evidently feel the sorrow, pain and distress we cause him. This spiritual personality is always behind our attitudes and actions, much as the devil is (v. 27).

CARING TIME

Begin by sharing any personal prayer requests and then answering the question:

"What would you like to change in the way you handle conflict with your spouse?"

Go around and let each couple pray for the couple on their right, remembering the concerns that have been shared. Start with this sentence:

"Dear God, I want to talk with you about my friend ____________."

Close by thanking God for bringing you together as a group and asking him to help you grow through the conflict and difficulties of marriage.

LEADER:

If applicable, have the group use the extra space on this page for group prayer requests.

SESSION

4

Communicating Heart to Heart

OBJECTIVES

To develop an awareness of the basic aspects of communication.

To begin to build more effective communication skills.

To encourage transparency in communication.

To consider Jesus a model of communication.

THREE-PART AGENDA

ICE-BREAKER	ISSUE / BIBLE STUDY	CARING TIME
15 Minutes	45 Minutes	30 Minutes

OPTION: If you only have 60 minutes, divide this session into two sessions, with the Bible Study section for your next time together.

ICE-BREAKER

Pass out the Handout for this session or the course book to each person. Divide the group into subgroups of 4 to 6 to do the Ice-Breaker. (Photocopy pages 33 and 35 as needed.)

1. When you answer the phone at home, how do you usually say "Hello"?

❒ "Yo, speak to me."
❒ "Hello, this is ________________ speaking."
❒ "Top of the mornin' to you!"
❒ "Ev'nin', how may I help you?"
❒ "Doe residence, John speaking!"
❒ "Good day, I've got the time, if you've got the weather."
❒ other:____

2. My usual first greeting when I come home and meet my spouse is:

❒ "Hey, hey, I'm home!"
❒ "Hoo boy, what a day!"
❒ "Honey, what's for dinner?"
❒ "Honey, guess who's coming for dinner?"
❒ Hugs all around!
❒ "Hi, dear, any mail?"
❒ other:____________

INTRODUCTION TO THE ISSUE

LEADER:

• Summarize these remarks (in your own words) into a brief introduction (no longer than 5 minutes).

• Be careful not to read the entire presentation to the group.

• In your presentation cover the "Discuss the Issue" questions listed on Side One of the Handout.

One of the most efficient examples of communication ever heard comes from a line in a '60s love song: "Hello, I love you, won't you tell me your name?"

"Efficient?" you ask. You bet! The communicator has gone from introduction to intimacy in four words. And not only is it efficient, it is also quite thorough, as the information-seeking question at the end of the line indicates. The singer wants to know this person he has come to love!

In real life, the process of moving from one level of communication to the next usually takes more than one sentence. It also takes a slightly different order. According to Robert Munger, there are three levels of conversation:

- "Hello" talk (a surface exchange about things like weather and baseball);
- "Head" talk (an exchange of ideas, opinions and knowledge); and,
- "Heart" talk (a sharing of feelings, hopes, fears, joys, loves).[9]

The aim, therefore, when couples communicate, is to move from introductory to informational to intimate conversation.

Awareness

Awareness is the foundation of good communication. Unless I know myself and my partner (and unless I am conscious of the nature of the relationship that we have), I will forfeit the chance of entering into meaningful communication. Awareness, as defined in one dictionary, suggests that this is a state in which two or more people "share knowledge of something not generally known or apparent." Let's look at three types of awareness in more detail:

- **Self-awareness.** Self-awareness means knowing who we are, what we value, where we want to go in life as individuals. It has to do with being conscious of our own actions and attitudes.
- **Spouse-awareness.** Spouse-awareness means knowing the other person who has come to share life with us. Spouse-awareness begins to occur when one person seeks to understand another, and not just him/herself.
- **Interpersonal-awareness.** Interpersonal-awareness means discovering what it takes for two people to interact on a deep and personal level as a married couple.

Environment

Finding a good environment in which to communicate is a crucial factor in developing intimacy in conversations. Generally speaking, people don't share their life goals at football games. Nor do they express their deepest joys and fears in supermarkets. The environment of a crowded elevator stifles nearly all verbal conversation, and a shopping mall is a lousy place to propose marriage. To enable effective communication, find a good place for open expression of thoughts, feelings, convictions and hopes.

A second part of the communication environment has to do with the attitude we bring to the process. How do we approach each other? Are we open and receptive, or guarded and distracted at this time? Are these characteristics so well-established in us that they can be counted on to remain fixed, or do they show some prospect for change?

Insight into such issues only comes a little at a time as we seek to discover the sensitivities and personality traits of our spouse. A healthy communicating environment develops when we affirm the uniqueness, dignity and worth of the other person who has been brought into our life, and allow space for growth and change in both of us as we live together.

Previous conversations are another part of the communication environment. If my partner hits my hot button and we don't resolve the conflict that results, a barrier rises the next time we begin to talk. The longer we avoid the issue, the larger the barrier gets. Likewise, broken promises, critical comments, sweeping generalizations, and poorly concluded conversations all impact our ability to reestablish lines of communication. The environment has to be addressed.

A pastor offered the simplest solution to these barriers in the communication environment when he advised people: "Keep 'fessed up!" That means, keep bringing out into the open the sources of conflict you have caused. Confess them; ask for forgiveness. Don't drag out your conflicts over a long period of time.

How do couples develop communication that freely moves from the introductory to the intimate? Singing, "Hello, I love you, won't you tell me your name?" may not be a bad idea after all. If you attempt this approach, however, try the following: When you say "Hello," listen for the response. You may have to work on the environment before going further. When you ask, "Won't you tell me your name?" make sure you ask about other things such as interests, ideas and opinions as well. Be sure to respond in a flexible style to his or her comments. And when you say, "I love you," do so with a keen awareness of yourselves and this relationship.

SESSION FOUR HANDOUT: Marriage Enrichment

Communicating Heart to Heart

ICE-BREAKER / Groups of 4 to 6 / 15 Minutes

1. When you answer the phone at home, how do you usually say "Hello"?
   - ❒ "Yo, speak to me."
   - ❒ "Top of the mornin' to you!"
   - ❒ "Doe residence, John speaking!"
   - ❒ "Good day, I've got the time, if you've got the weather."
   - ❒ "Hello, this is ________speaking."
   - ❒ "Ev'nin', how may I help you?"
   - ❒ other:__________________

2. My usual first greeting when I come home and meet my spouse is:
   - ❒ "Hey, hey, I'm home!"
   - ❒ "Hoo boy, what a day!"
   - ❒ "Honey, what's for dinner?"
   - ❒ "Honey, guess who's coming for dinner?"
   - ❒ Hugs all around!
   - ❒ "Hi, dear, any mail?"
   - ❒ other:_______________________

DISCUSS THE ISSUE / Same Groups / 20 Minutes

After a brief introduction by the leader, take turns sharing your responses to the following questions.

1. In your opinion, what proportion of the typical married couple's communication is spent at each of these levels?
   "Hello" talk _____% "Head" talk _____% "Heart" talk _____%

2. For you and yours, what is the best environment for an intimate conversation?
   - ❒ on a long trip in the car
   - ❒ while taking a walk together
   - ❒ with our heads on the same pillow in bed
   - ❒ in a quiet restaurant
   - ❒ at the kitchen table
   - ❒ other:__________________

3. What "environmental factor" have you worked on the most in your communication as a couple?
   - ❒ PLACE—We've got some great retreat spots where we can talk undisturbed.
   - ❒ PERSONAL RESPONSIVENESS—We've learned a lot about openness and acceptance.
   - ❒ PRESERVING OUR ENVIRONMENT—For the most part we remain " 'fessed up" and forgiving.

4. Dennis Rainey defines transparent communication as "sharing who you are; sharing your heart; complete emotional and personal truthfulness."[10] Thus defined, how would you rate your progress toward transparent communication?
   - ❒ We're covering up more than we're exposing.
   - ❒ We're still pretty cautious about this.
   - ❒ We're becoming vulnerable with each other.
   - ❒ We can gaze into each other's heart.

INTRODUCTION TO THE BIBLE STUDY

The relationship between Jesus and his first disciples grew out of a very ordinary conversation. Two men followed the recommendation of John the Baptist and decided they would like to meet Jesus. Jesus saw them coming and asked the easy question, "What do you want?" The two men responded at the same introductory level, "Teacher, where are you staying?" Jesus, in turn, said, "Come and you will see." By the end of the day, another friend is introduced; the next day two others make his acquaintance. In the course of the conversation, Jesus makes several "heart" comments that strike right to the core of the person. For example, he gives Peter insight into who he (Peter) truly is; and for Nathanael, he affirms him in his essence.

Let's look at these first conversations between Jesus and those who would become his disciples to see what levels of communication were reached, and to reflect on what these conversations teach us about communicating with each other and with Jesus.

ICE-BREAKER FOR TWO-SESSION OPTION

If you are doing the Bible Study as a separate session, start off this session by dividing this group into subgroups of 4 to 6 and answering the following questions. Photocopy and give this to the group.

1. How did you tend to communicate as a child?
- ❒ spent a lot of time talking to a few friends
- ❒ didn't talk much but played hard
- ❒ shared secrets with my best friend
- ❒ read a lot but didn't talk about it much
- ❒ talked a lot to my Mom (or Dad)
- ❒ didn't like to talk much
- ❒ chattered to anyone who would listen
- ❒ other:______________________________

2. As an adult, what do you feel most comfortable talking about?
- ❒ ideas
- ❒ feelings
- ❒ activities

3. What is your strength in conversation?
- ❒ listening
- ❒ making a few telling comments
- ❒ making others feel good
- ❒ letting others talk
- ❒ talking with energy
- ❒ humor
- ❒ wry remarks
- ❒ other:____________

SESSION FOUR BIBLE STUDY

35 The next day John was there again with two of his disciples. 36 When he saw Jesus passing by, he said, "Look, the Lamb of God!"

37 When the two disciples heard him say this, they followed Jesus. 38 Turning around, Jesus saw them following and asked, "What do you want?"

They said, "Rabbi" (which means Teacher), "where are you staying?"

39 "Come," he replied, "and you will see."

So they went and saw where he was staying, and spent that day with him. It was about the tenth hour.

40 Andrew, Simon Peter's brother, was one of the two who heard what John had said and who had followed Jesus. 41 The first thing Andrew did was to find his brother Simon and tell him, "We have found the Messiah" (that is, the Christ). 42 And he brought him to Jesus.

Jesus looked at him and said, "You are Simon son of John. You will be called Cephas" (which, when translated, is Peter).

43 The next day Jesus decided to leave for Galilee. Finding Philip, he said to him, "Follow me."

44 Philip, like Andrew and Peter, was from the town of Bethsaida. 45 Philip found Nathanael and told him, "We have found the one Moses wrote about in the Law, and about whom the prophets also wrote—Jesus of Nazareth, the son of Joseph."

46 "Nazareth! Can anything good come from there?" Nathanael asked.

"Come and see," said Philip.

47 When Jesus saw Nathanael approaching, he said of him, "Here is a true Israelite, in whom there is nothing false."

48 "How do you know me?" Nathanael asked.

Jesus answered, "I saw you while you were still under the fig tree before Philip called you." 49 Then Nathanael declared, "Rabbi, you are the Son of God; you are the King of Israel."

50 Jesus said, "You believe because I told you I saw you under the fig tree. You shall see greater things than that."

John 1:35–50

1. What drew you to Jesus?
❒ the influence of my parents
❒ the changed life of a friend
❒ historical evidence that he is God's Son
❒ my own personal yearnings
❒ I'm still investigating.
❒ other:____________________

2. What does it mean to you to communicate heart to heart with Jesus?
❒ to ask questions without feeling embarrassed
❒ to share what's going on in my life in an honest way
❒ to receive an encouraging word from him
❒ other:____

3. How does communicating heart to heart with Jesus help you communicate heart to heart with your spouse?

4. On a scale from 1 (low) to 10 (high) how are you and Jesus getting along? Where do you need to grow in your spiritual life?

REFERENCE NOTES

John 1:35–50

1:35–42 This seemingly insignificant conversation is full of allusions to the meaning of discipleship. The author often veils theological truth in ordinary language.

1:35 *two of his disciples.* One was Andrew, Simon Peter's brother (v. 40). Tradition holds the other was John, the author of this Gospel. Both were disciples of John the Baptist, and now become disciples of Jesus (v. 37).

1:36 *Lamb of God.* This title used by John the Baptist for Jesus must be understood in the context of the Old Testament sacrificial system, in which an animal (such as a lamb at Passover) was sacrificed as a substitute for the judgment rightfully due to the person who made the sacrifice for his or her sin. Abraham is spared having to kill his son when God provides a lamb in the place of Isaac (Gen. 22:8,13). The Hebrews are delivered from destruction at the hands of the Egyptians when God provides the Passover lamb, symbolizing their salvation (Ex. 12:3–17). It is a Lamb led to slaughter, bearing the sins of many, who thus fulfills the role of the Suffering Servant (Isa. 53).

1:38 *What do you want?* Not "who" but "what"—indicating that these first would-be disciples (as with most others engaged in a spiritual pursuit), are looking for some *thing*; imagine their surprise when that thing turns out to be a *person.*

Rabbi. Rabbis were teachers who gathered disciples around them. Normally they were trained by other rabbis, and teaching consisted of passing along the heritage of the past to the new students. One of the things that puzzled the religious leaders about Jesus was that they knew he had never studied under a rabbi, yet he seemed to be well-versed in the Scriptures (7:15).

1:39 *Come ... see.* This is an invitation by Jesus for these followers to enter into discipleship with him.

the tenth hour. Days and nights were divided into 12 hours. Day began about 6 a.m. our time, so this was about 4 p.m. In the absence of clocks, time references are naturally estimates rather than precise accounts.

1:42 *Cephas.* The Aramaic name, Cephas, and the Greek name, Peter, both mean "rock." Although Peter often seemed unstable during Jesus' time with him (John 18:15–17,25–27), after the Ascension Peter became the chief spokesman for the apostles (Acts 2:14).

1:47 *a true Israelite.* Jesus' greeting implies an awareness of the spiritual motivations of Nathanael reflected in that he, unlike Israel as a whole, came to him.

1:48 *I saw you.* This accents the supernatural knowledge of Jesus.

CARING TIME

Close by sharing prayer requests and praying for one another. Ask for God's help on developing more heart-to-heart communication with your spouse in the coming week. Begin by having each group member answer the question:

"How can we help you in prayer this week?"

Conclude your prayer time by reading Psalm 139:1-4,23-24 together:

O Lord, you have searched me
and you know me.
You know when I sit and when I rise;
you perceive my thoughts from afar.
You discern my going out and my lying down;
you are familiar with all my ways.
Before a word is on my tongue
you know it completely, O Lord.

Search me, O God, and know my heart;
test me and know my anxious thoughts.
See if there is any offensive way in me,
and lead me in the way everlasting.

LEADER:

If applicable, have the group use the extra space on this page for group prayer requests.

SESSION

5

Sexual Intimacy

OBJECTIVES

To present a positive view of sexuality in marriage.

To identify some areas for growth in sexual communication.

To affirm each other in the midst of the learning and loving.

To consider what the Bible says about intimacy in marriage.

THREE-PART AGENDA

ICE-BREAKER	**ISSUE / BIBLE STUDY**	**CARING TIME**
15 Minutes	45 Minutes	30 Minutes

OPTION: If you only have 60 minutes, divide this session into two sessions, with the Bible Study section for your next time together.

ICE-BREAKER

Pass out the Handout for this session or the course book to each person. Divide the group into subgroups of 4 to 6 to do the Ice-Breaker. (Photocopy pages 41 and 43 as needed.)

1. Are these statements true or false, in your opinion?
- The average person thinks about sex 6–7 times per day.
- On the average, a couple's sexual attraction toward each other increases once they marry.
- Talking about sex in marriage is less difficult in our generation than in our parents' generation.
- Sex is more an extension of a relationship than a separate aspect of it.

2. In your opinion, why don't people talk much about married sex?
- ❒ Who said so? Why just last night ...
- ❒ What's there to talk about it? If it ain't broke, don't fix it.
- ❒ Many people don't think there is sex after marriage.
- ❒ Married sex is too sacred to talk about in mixed company.
- ❒ Married sex is okay for Oprah to talk about, but too embarrassing for church groups.
- ❒ other:______________________________

INTRODUCTION TO THE ISSUE

LEADER:

• Summarize these remarks (in your own words) into a brief introduction (no longer than 5 minutes).

• Be careful not to read the entire presentation to the group.

• In your presentation cover the "Discuss the Issue" questions listed on Side One of the Handout.

There's been a revolution around here. What was once too personal to discuss in public has become the topic of talk shows from coast to coast. What was once only hinted at in movies that our parents forbade us to watch is vividly portrayed in prime time television night after night. We see this new openness to discussing sex in everything from scientific surveys, statistical reports, popular magazines, to best-selling books.

The comments of two newly married people provides a clear illustration of the changes which have taken place in the last generation. When asked to look back on the first night of her married life, here's what a 63-year-old woman, who married in 1943, wrote on her questionnaire:

> We had a small wedding and spent our wedding night at the Waldorf-Astoria. Our first real intimate contact was taking a bath together at night—and it was such a thrill to be able to spend the night together! Sleeping together was thrilling enough for the first night! We saved the BIG DEAL for the second night.

A 26-year-old groom, who had lived with his bride for six months before marriage, wrote this:

> We got to our hotel room and started counting the checks we were given at the wedding. By the time I finished, she had fallen asleep. It was no big deal.

Between these extremes of "big deal" and "no big deal" are most other couples. Forty percent of couples say that sex is very important to marriage, and 57 percent say sex is somewhat important to marriage. What is clear is that with all the talk about sex, almost everyone feels that they are entitled to a fulfilling sex life.

However, not all these high expectations are being realized. A full 25 percent of couples in their first year of marriage surveyed by Arond and Pauker indicated that they were experiencing sexual problems. Another 22 percent of the females and 11 percent of the males said that they experienced a fading of passion or lack of sexual drive. They reported that a 50 percent drop-off in sexual activity had become the norm by their first anniversary.

Perhaps we ought to call an end to the sexual revolution while we work out healthy views of sexuality! Failing that, it is important for us to work at building quality sexual relationships with our partners.

Arond and Pauker's discussion of married sex ends on an upbeat note with a list of seven ingredients of good married sex.

Seven Ingredients of Good Married Sex

- **Make sex a priority.** Decide that sex is essential to your marriage. Make appointments to meet in bed. Don't put it off because other things seem more important at the time.
- **Compliment your spouse.** Tell him or her often: "I love you ... I need you ... I respect you ... I want you ... I can't live without you." Sex flourishes when love and positive feelings are reinforced and secure.
- **Pretend you're still dating.** Dress up. Splash on that special fragrance. Be considerate of each other the way you used to be. Remember the way you used to try to impress each other. Do it again.
- **Be romantic.** Whether it's bubble bath, a bouquet of flowers, something sexy to wear in bed, or a scented candle lit in the bedroom, build a mood for romance.
- **Communicate—don't complain—about sex.** Sex is usually the most difficult subject to talk about, because doing so reveals so much about who we are and how we feel about our partner. Therefore, your best communication abilities must be offered. Give positive feedback; show your mate what you like; listen to your mate's ideas; talk about improving lovemaking when both of you are comfortable talking about it. Be suggestive rather than direct, if that is more effective. Never make accusations, and avoid hammering home the same point repeatedly or maliciously.
- **Break the routine.** Change the pace with variety of time, place and style. Surprise your partner. Think of ways to please your partner and enhance your lovemaking.
- **Keep a balanced perspective.** Remember that sex is just one part of your relationship. Working to improve your relationship in other areas will benefit your sex life also. If you're upset about sexual problems, focus on the positive aspects of your marriage. The closer you both feel to each other, the easier it will be to share your sexual needs and desires.[11]

The Secret to Intimacy

Marriage enables couples to express their needs and desires, fears and fantasies with a confidence that they won't be rejected. When a person says to his or her spouse, "I'm committed to you for as long as we both shall live," the other spouse can reveal what might otherwise be too fearful to disclose. It is this open expression of commitment which underlies the concluding words in the story of Adam and Eve: "The man and his wife were both naked and they felt no shame" (Gen. 2:25).

SESSION FIVE HANDOUT: Marriage Enrichment

Sexual Intimacy

ICE-BREAKER / Groups of 4 to 6 / 15 Minutes

1. Are these statements true or false, in your opinion?
   - The average person thinks about sex 6–7 times per day.
   - On the average, a couple's sexual attraction toward each other increases once they marry.
   - Talking about sex in marriage is less difficult in our generation than in our parents' generation.
   - Sex is more an extension of a relationship than a separate aspect of it.

2. In your opinion, why don't people talk much about married sex?
   - ❒ Who said so? Why just last night ...
   - ❒ What's there to talk about it? If it ain't broke, don't fix it.
   - ❒ Many people don't think there is sex after marriage.
   - ❒ Married sex is too sacred to talk about in mixed company.
   - ❒ Married sex is okay for Oprah to talk about, but too embarrassing for church groups.
   - ❒ other:____

DISCUSS THE ISSUE / Same Groups / 20 Minutes

After a brief introduction by the leader, take turns sharing your responses to the following questions.

1. Which of the seven ingredients of good married sex would you recommend in order to maximize your sexual happiness as a couple?
   - ❒ Make sex a priority.
   - ❒ Pretend you're still dating.
   - ❒ Break the routine.
   - ❒ Communicate—don't complain—about sex.
   - ❒ Compliment your spouse.
   - ❒ Be romantic.
   - ❒ Keep a balanced perspective.

2. From your perspective, which of these word pairs has the most in common?
   - ❒ sex and romance
   - ❒ sex and marriage
   - ❒ sex and oneness
   - ❒ sex and "serendipity" (not the book publisher!)
   - ❒ sex and passion
   - ❒ sex and childbearing

3. Make a mental note about something positive you would like to say to your spouse about the sexual life you share. Decide when you will present this gift of affirmation.

INTRODUCTION TO THE BIBLE STUDY

The Bible has been called "the world's most reliable textbook on sex. No book deals more forthrightly with the subject." Both sexual norms and sexual deviations are described with straightforward explicitness in the Bible. By linking sexual happiness and moral integrity, the Bible is able to present sexual behavior as pure, good and worthy of celebration. Where there has been sexual sin, the Bible declares God's readiness to forgive and restore those who come to him for help.[12]

The place of sexuality in married life is described in many places in the Bible. One of the most helpful passages on sex and oneness is found in 1 Corinthians 6:12–7:5. Here the apostle Paul responds to questions asked by the young Christians in Corinth about the appropriateness of sex in and outside of marriage.

ICE-BREAKER FOR TWO-SESSION OPTION

If you are doing the Bible Study as a separate session, start off this session by dividing this group into subgroups of 4 to 6 and answering the following questions. Photocopy and give this to the group.

1. When did you receive your first talk about sex? What was your response?

2. Did your mom or dad (or a good friend) say anything on the eve of your wedding to calm your fear of that "oh-so-delicate" subject of sex? Can you share what you were told?

3. What "snapshot" of your first six months of marriage reflects the intimate side of your relationship? (Tell the story behind the picture.)

❐ painting the new apartment, in bib overalls
❐ candlelit dinner for two, keeping the courtship going
❐ staring bleary-eyed from behind a stack of school books
❐ staring bleary-eyed from behind a stack of dishes
❐ dressed down and holding hands at the church picnic
❐ all suited up and holding hands at an office coffee break
❐ dancing the night away
❐ bundled up in ski wear
❐ decked out in fancy formal wear
❐ trying on maternity clothes
❐ other:____

SESSION FIVE BIBLE STUDY

*[12]"Everything is permissible for me"—but not everything is beneficial.
"Everything is permissible for me"—but I will not be mastered by anything.
[13]"Food for the stomach and the stomach for food"—but God will destroy them both. The
body is not meant for sexual immorality, but for the Lord, and the Lord for the body. [14]By
his power God raised the Lord from the dead, and he will raise us also. [15]Do you not know
that your bodies are members of Christ himself? Shall I then take the members of Christ
and unite them with a prostitute? Never! [16]Do you not know that he who unites himself with
a prostitute is one with her in body? For it is said, "The two will become one flesh." [17]But
he who unites himself with the Lord is one with him in spirit.*

*[18]Flee from sexual immorality. All other sins a man commits are outside his body, but
he who sins sexually sins against his own body. [19]Do you not know that your body is a tem-
ple of the Holy Spirit, who is in you, whom you have received from God? You are not your
own; [20]you were bought at a price. Therefore honor God with your body.*

*7 Now for the matters you wrote about: It is good for a man not to marry. [2]But since
there is so much immorality, each man should have his own wife, and each woman
her own husband. [3]The husband should fulfill his marital duty to his wife, and likewise the
wife to her husband. [4]The wife's body does not belong to her alone but also to her hus-
band. In the same way, the husband's body does not belong to him alone but also to his
wife. [5]Do not deprive each other except by mutual consent and for a time, so that you may
devote yourselves to prayer. Then come together again so that Satan will not tempt you
because of your lack of self-control.*

1 Corinthians 6:12–7:5

1. What statement in this passage do you find most striking or surprising?

2. How do sexuality and spirituality relate to each other in this passage?

3. What does it mean to you to realize that your body does not belong to you alone, and that your spouse's body does not belong to him or her alone?
   ❒ It makes me feel united to my spouse.
   ❒ It makes me want to learn to be more unselfish.
   ❒ It makes me feel a little threatened.
   ❒ It makes me feel secure.

4. How do you arrive at "mutual consent" in sexual matters?
   ❒ We work at listening to each other's feelings, both positive and negative.
   ❒ We remind each other that sex is not our god.
   ❒ We agree never to use sex as a weapon.
   ❒ We realize intimacy does not always express itself sexually.
   ❒ other:____

REFERENCE NOTES

1 Corinthians 6:12–7:5

6:12 ***"Everything is permissible for me."*** This was probably the slogan of a libertarian party at Corinth which felt that since the body was insignificant (in comparison with the "spirit"), it did not matter what one did. Paul takes issue with the way the slogan has come to be used: i.e., as an excuse for indulgent and promiscuous behavior. He argues that while everything may be permissible, not everything is good (much less beneficial).

6:15 Since the body of the Christian belongs to the Lord and is for his use, it is inconceivable (*"Never"*) that it be handed over to a prostitute.

prostitute. Paul may not have in mind prostitutes in general (they were numerous in a port city like Corinth), but temple prostitutes in particular. The Corinthians may have been arguing for the "right" to engage in sexually oriented religious activities.

6:16 ***unites.*** "Joined together." In its literal use, this word refers to gluing things together. In its metaphorical sense, it points to the strong bonding between two people that takes place as a result of intercourse. Intercourse is not merely an inconsequential physical act. In fact, it is akin to the bonding between the believer and the Lord, as Paul shows in verse 17 (where he uses this same word). Such uniting with a prostitute makes the two one flesh. This stands in contrast to becoming one in spirit with God (v. 17).

7:1 ***to marry.*** This translation of Greek text is probably wrong. The phrase is literally, "to touch a woman," and is a common euphemism for sexual intercourse. "Nowhere in the ancient world is this phrase used to mean 'get married' " (Fee).

7:3–4 Paul now gives the reasons for his views. There is to be complete mutuality within marriage in the matter of sexual rights. This statement stands in sharp contrast to the consensus of the first century, which understood that it was the husband alone who had sexual rights and the wife simply submitted to him. For Paul, marriage is a partnership.

7:5 This is the negative form of the commandment in verses 3–4. Abstinence is allowed under two conditions: both partners agree, and it is for a limited time. The purpose of such abstinence is prayer.

deprive. This word could be translated "rob." For one partner to opt out of sexual relations is a form of robbery, and is certainly not an act of "spirituality" (as some might have been saying).

lack of self-control. Paul assumes that a couple would not be married in the first place if they did not feel any sexual desire, and thus they ought to fulfill such desires legitimately, lest they be tempted to adultery.

CARING TIME

Take time now to share any concerns and pray for one another. Have each group member answer the question:

"How can we help you in prayer this week?"

Then, move into prayer. At the close, join hands and pray this prayer together.

"Dear God, thank you for the gift of sexuality.
Guide each couple here in finding the
right path to an intimacy that includes
sexuality, spirituality, and the open
sharing of feelings. Amen."

LEADER:

If applicable, have the group use the extra space on this page for group prayer requests.

SESSION

6

Enjoying Life Together

OBJECTIVES

To help couples identify and appreciate what they have in common, as well as what is uniquely his or hers.

To explore both positive and negative factors affecting intimacy.

THREE-PART AGENDA

ICE-BREAKER	**ISSUE / BIBLE STUDY**	**CARING TIME**
15 Minutes	45 Minutes	30 Minutes

OPTION: If you only have 60 minutes, divide this session into two sessions, with the Bible Study section for your next time together.

ICE-BREAKER

Pass out the Handout for this session or the course book to each person. Divide the group into subgroups of 4 to 6 to do the Ice-Breaker. (Photocopy pages 49 and 51 as needed.)

Which of the following interests do you both have in common? Put a "B" (both) next to these items. Put an "H" (husband) next to those items which interest only the husband and a "W" (wife) next to those items which interest only the wife. Use the two blank lines to add items you are both interested in, but which are not on the list.

_____ garage sales
_____ bicycling
_____ reading the business page
_____ jogging / exercise / walking
_____ balancing the checkbook
_____ visiting an art museum
_____ visiting a zoo
_____ attending class reunions
_____ attending sporting events
_____ other:_______________

_____ fishing
_____ caring for a pet
_____ shopping at the mall
_____ watching television
_____ eating out
_____ attending auto shows
_____ gardening
_____ reading
_____ conversation
_____ other:_______________

Add up all the interests both of you marked with a "B."

- If you have a score over 10, you deserve the Birds of a Feather Award.
- If you have a score of 5–10, you deserve the Two Turtledoves Award.
- If you have a score of 0–5, you deserve the Jonathan Livingston Seagull Solo Award.

INTRODUCTION TO THE ISSUE

LEADER:

• Summarize these remarks (in your own words) into a brief introduction (no longer than 5 minutes).

• Be careful not to read the entire presentation to the group.

• In your presentation cover the "Discuss the Issue" questions listed on Side One of the Handout.

Ask any engaged couple why they've decided to marry. Undoubtedly you'll hear some variation on the theme: "We just want to be together; we feel so close; we have so many things in common." Togetherness is what marriage is supposed to be all about. But what do we mean by these kinds of statements? Do we mean that ...

- we form a dependency bond with each other?
- we build a "lean-on-each-other" relationship?
- we do everything together?
- we share all interests and experiences with each other?
- we have all our friends in common?

While some couples may opt for this total intimacy approach, others would feel smothered by it. In fact, there seems to be a tension in most of us between our desire for intimacy and our desire for distance. We want to experience connection, and yet we also want to experience separation; we want to be dependent, but at the same time we long to remain autonomous.

How we resolve this tension depends upon a number of interrelated factors. Arond and Pauker have identified six primary factors affecting our attitudes about intimacy:

- early childhood experience
- being male or female
- personality type
- role models for intimacy
- experiences in previous relationships
- stage in life

Sorting through these factors can play a significant role in determining the level of intimacy you will share as a couple. The following are examples of each factor:

- **Childhood Issues.** One spouse may wish to recreate the sense of closeness and security he or she had (or wanted) as a child, while the other spouse still may be trying to escape from an overbearing parent. Without knowing this background, spouses may feel either unloved (in the first instance) or smothered (in the second instance).
- **Gender Differences.** Simply being male or female tends to have an impact on the level of closeness you will desire and accept, especially in the early stages of marriage. In Western culture, separation is commonly associated with the development of a masculine identity, but it is not required in the formation of a feminine identity. It follows that intimacy may be more threatening to a man ("If I am too close to her, have I really become a man?"), while separation may be more threatening to a woman ("Why would he want to spend time apart from me—am I somehow not good enough?").
- **Personality Type.** Discovering the distinctives of each spouse's personality plays an important part in establishing a couple's level of

intimacy. The Meyers-Briggs Temperament Indicator is a well-known test that helps people discover the degree to which they are extroverts or introverts, how much they rely on sensory observation or intuition in making decisions, whether they are primarily thinkers or feelers, and whether they prefer organization or spontaneity. It is interesting to note how often young couples have one of those "Aha!" moments of discovery when they share the results of such tests with each other.

- **Role Models.** Each individual's role models have a significant impact on his or her approach to intimacy. We tend to pattern our relationships after those relationships we have seen in the past. If we have had different types of role models (and if these role models are not disclosed to each other), the nature and level of intimacy that is sought may vary greatly.

- **Previous Relationships.** Similarly, experiences in previous relationships have an impact on intimacy. In some cases, couples need to seek professional help to sort out the issues of the past that have not been fully resolved prior to marriage.

- **Stage in Life.** Another factor in determining the level of intimacy acceptable to both spouses concerns the stage in life of the marriage partners. Life cycle issues are age-determined. For example, a man at midlife is moving away from his activist, outward-oriented lifestyle to a more inward life, and as a result has strong needs for emotional intimacy. Life cycle issues also relate to the pressures of the moment. If one or both spouses are on a high-intensity career track at the time of their marriage, this will most likely have a substantial impact on intimacy.[13]

Once spouses know the impact of these factors, they can begin a process of achieving a close relationship that is satisfying to both of them. David Mace calls this process "mutual adaptation."

According to Mace, "It (mutual adaptation) means strengthening the affinities and resolving, as far as possible, the hostilities. It is a difficult art calling for skill and patience. But it can be learned; and those who learn it have in their hands the means to raise their involvement with each other as marriage partners to the highest level of which they as a couple are capable without violating the sanctity of each other's personhood."[14]

Moving Toward a Vital Relationship

No couple is locked into the style of marriage they are presently experiencing. People can and do change. The key is in the choosing and in the willingness to work in an honest, loving and committed way to bring about change. It is simply a matter of deciding to change our behavior and doing something about it. "If anyone is in Christ, he [or she] is a new creation"—and this applies to marriage.

SESSION SIX HANDOUT: Marriage Enrichment

Enjoying Life Together

ICE-BREAKER / Groups of 4 to 6 / 15 Minutes

Which of the following interests do you both have in common? Put a "B" (both) next to these items. Put an "H" (husband) next to those items which interest only the husband and a "W" (wife) next to those items which interest only the wife. Use the two blank lines to add items you are both interested in, but which are not on the list.

_____ garage sales
_____ bicycling
_____ reading the business page
_____ jogging / exercise / walking
_____ balancing the checkbook
_____ visiting an art museum
_____ visiting a zoo
_____ attending class reunions
_____ attending sporting events
_____ other:_______________

_____ fishing
_____ caring for a pet
_____ shopping at the mall
_____ watching television
_____ eating out
_____ attending auto shows
_____ gardening
_____ reading
_____ conversation
_____ other:_______________

Add up all the interests both of you marked with a "B."
- If you have a score over 10, you deserve the Birds of a Feather Award.
- If you have a score of 5–10, you deserve the Two Turtledoves Award.
- If you have a score of 0–5, you deserve the Jonathan Livingston Seagull Solo Award.

DISCUSS THE ISSUE / Same Groups / 20 Minutes

After a brief introduction by the leader, take turns sharing your responses to the following questions.

1. In your opinion, what is the greatest hindrance to preserving marital togetherness?
❒ unresolved hurts from childhood
❒ inability to overcome male/female stereotypes about intimacy
❒ personality clashes
❒ poor models of intimacy on which to build
❒ previous disappointments in close relationships
❒ different stages in the life cycle

2. How far have you traveled in togetherness (i.e., the process of strengthening what you have in common and resolving differences)? Which of these apply to your relationship?
❒ We've strengthened our common interests.
❒ We've resolved some hostilities.
❒ We've raised our mutual involvement to a higher level.
❒ We've smothered our individual lives and need to draw back a little.
❒ We've drawn back too much and aren't connected enough.

INTRODUCTION TO THE BIBLE STUDY

Life together is one of the great purposes for which we were created. God identified man's aloneness as "not good," and stepped in to remedy the problem by creating woman to be with him (Gen. 2:15–25). Reflecting on their joyful companionship, the writer of Genesis says, in effect, "This is the reason a man leaves home! We've been made for intimacy!" (Gen. 2:24). The privilege of togetherness is a great one. "How very good and pleasant it is when kindred live together in unity!" (Ps. 133:1, NRSV). Life together is as sacred as an ordination ceremony, a commissioning service, or the occasion in which one takes the oath of office. When we commit ourselves to life together in marriage, we are being "set apart for service to one another."

In a series of brief exhortations, the apostle Paul instructs us in the art of living together.

ICE-BREAKER FOR TWO-SESSION OPTION

If you are doing the Bible Study as a separate session, start off this session by dividing this group into subgroups of 4 to 6 and answering the following questions. Photocopy and give this to the group.

1. Describe your first date together. Where did you go? What did you do? What did you talk about? How did you feel?

2. Describe the when, the where and the feelings associated with as many of the following types of dates as you can recall:

   CHEAP DATES: For example: at the zoo, people-watching, at the beach, sitting *outside* the concert hall, romance in the park, library mania, biking or hiking.

   MODERATE DATES: dinner and a movie, a day at an amusement park, going *to* a concert, taking lessons in a new skill/hobby.

   SPORTS DATES: football tailgate party and game, golf outing, ballroom dance contest, sailing, skiing, horseback riding, bowling league.

   OUTRAGEOUSLY EXPENSIVE DATES: hot air balloon ride, yacht cruise, private showing of a first-release movie, helicopter ride.

   GROUP DATES: rehearsal dinner, wedding reception/dance, camping trip, theme night, parade (make a float, pull it together), group dinner, gourmet club, bridge club, birthday party.

3. When you think of where you'd like to go (and what you'd like to do) on your next "date" this month, what scene comes to mind? Any of the above suggestions? Something more creative?

SESSION SIX BIBLE STUDY

***12** Therefore, I urge you, brothers, in view of God's mercy, to offer your bodies as living sacrifices, holy and pleasing to God—this is your spiritual act of worship. 2 Do not conform any longer to the pattern of this world, but be transformed by the renewing of your mind. Then you will be able to test and approve what God's will is—his good, pleasing and perfect will.*

3 For by the grace given me I say to every one of you: Do not think of yourself more highly than you ought, but rather think of yourself with sober judgment, in accordance with the measure of faith God has given you. 4 Just as each of us has one body with many members, and these members do not all have the same function, 5 so in Christ we who are many form one body, and each member belongs to all the others. 6 We have different gifts, according to the grace given us. If a man's gift is prophesying, let him use it in proportion to his faith. 7 If it is serving, let him serve; if it is teaching, let him teach; 8 if it is encouraging, let him encourage; if it is contributing to the needs of others, let him give generously; if it is leadership, let him govern diligently; if it is showing mercy, let him do it cheerfully.

9 Love must be sincere. Hate what is evil; cling to what is good. 10 Be devoted to one another in brotherly love. Honor one another above yourselves. 11 Never be lacking in zeal, but keep your spiritual fervor, serving the Lord. 12 Be joyful in hope, patient in affliction, faithful in prayer. 13 Share with God's people who are in need. Practice hospitality.

14 Bless those who persecute you; bless and do not curse. 15 Rejoice with those who rejoice; mourn with those who mourn. 16 Live in harmony with one another. Do not be proud, but be willing to associate with people of low position. Do not be conceited.

17 Do not repay anyone evil for evil. Be careful to do what is right in the eyes of everybody. 18 If it is possible, as far as it depends on you, live at peace with everyone. 19 Do not take revenge, my friends, but leave room for God's wrath, for it is written: "It is mine to avenge; I will repay," says the Lord.

Romans 12:1–19

1. In this series of exhortations, what stands out to you the most as a principle for helping married couples live together in harmony?

2. What harms the development of life together the most?
- ❐ when we refuse to let go of the world's pattern of relating
- ❐ when we think more highly of ourselves than we ought
- ❐ when we maintain a sense of independence from each other
- ❐ when we desire to get revenge for offenses
- ❐ other:______________________________

3. On a scale from 1 to 10—1 being "needs work" and 10 being "doing great"—where are you in each of these relationships?
- my relationship with God
- my relationship with my spouse
- my relationship with myself
- my relationship with others

4. What's the next step for you in drawing closer to your spouse?

REFERENCE NOTES

Romans 12:1–19

12:2 *Do not conform.* Literally, "stop allowing yourself to be conformed." Believers are no longer helpless victims of natural and supernatural forces which would shape them into a distorted pattern; rather they now have the ability to resist such powers.

be transformed. The force of the verb is: "continue to let yourself be transformed"; i.e., a continuous action by the Holy Spirit which goes on for a lifetime.

renewing of your mind. Develop a spiritual sensitivity and perception—learn to look at life on the basis of God's view of reality.

test and approve. Christians are called to a responsible freedom of choice and action, based on the inner renewing work of the Holy Spirit.

12:6 *gifts.* Those endowments given by God to every believer by grace, to be used in God's service.

12:9 *Love.* The Greek word here is *agape*—self-giving action on behalf of others made possible by God's Spirit.

sincere. Genuine, not counterfeit or showy. It is possible to pretend (even to one's self) to love others.

12:10 *brotherly love.* A second word for love is used here, *philadelphia,* denoting the tender affection found in families, now said to be appropriate to those in the church—which is the Christian's new family.

Honor. Since other Christians are in union with Christ, they are to be honored.

12:12 What makes it possible to endure affliction is joyful hope in one's inheritance in the age to come, coupled with daily, continuous prayer.

12:13 To be"renewed" is not just an interior matter of mind and emotions, but involves concrete outer action such as giving to those in need and blessing those who persecute us.

12:16 Christians ought to provide a model of harmony for the world around them. Avoiding haughtiness, they ought to put in its place unself-conscious association with all types of people.

12:17 *Do not repay anyone evil for evil.* A common Christian teaching. See 1 Thessalonians 5:15 and 1 Peter 3:4. Christians are called upon to do not just what the consensus calls "good," but those things that are inherently "good." These deeds will be recognized as such by those of good will.

CARING TIME

Share prayer requests and then have everyone answer the question:

"How do you need God's help in drawing closer to your spouse?"

Have each group member end their prayer by thanking God for the togetherness that can keep growing and building within their marriage.

Conclude your prayer time by reading together the words of Jesus in John 17:20-23:

"My prayer is not for them alone.
I pray also for those who will believe in me
through their message,that all of them may
be one, Father, just as you are
in me and I am in you.
May they also be in us so that the world
may believe that you have sent me.
I have given them the glory that you gave me,
that they may be one as we are one:
I in them and you in me.
May they be brought to complete unity to
let the world knowthat you sent me and have
loved them even as you have loved me."

LEADER:

If applicable, have the group use the extra space on this page for group prayer requests.

SESSION

7

Serving Together

OBJECTIVES

To explore what's involved in serving together as husbands and wives.

To consider the New Testament example of Priscilla and Aquila, who modeled what serving together means.

To decide on the next step, now that this course is drawing to a close.

THREE-PART AGENDA

ISSUE / BIBLE STUDY	ICE-BREAKER	CARING TIME
45 Minutes	15 Minutes	30 Minutes

NOTE: The agenda is reversed and there is no two-session option.

ICE-BREAKER

We recommend that you use the ice-breaker at the close of this session—as part of the Evaluation / Caring time. This affirmation exercise is on the back of the Handout.

NOTE: Ice-Breaker goes last with Evaluation / Caring Time.

Musical Instruments. If you had to create an orchestra out of your group, who would you nominate for these instruments? Read over the list and pick an instrument that best describes how you feel about each person in this group. Then ask one person to listen while the others tell this person which instrument they chose for them. Go around the circle so that everyone is affirmed.

ANGELIC HARP: Soft, gentle, melodious, wooing with heavenly sounds.

OLD-FASHIONED WASHBOARD: Nonconforming, childlike and fun.

PLAYER PIANO: Mischievous, raucous, honky-tonk—delightfully carefree.

KETTLE DRUM: Strong, vibrant, commanding when needed but usually in background.

PASSIONATE CASTANET: Full of Spanish fervor—intense and always upbeat.

more ⟶

STRADIVARIUS VIOLIN: Priceless, exquisite, soul-piercing—with the touch of the Master.

FLUTTERING FLUTE: Tender, lighthearted, wide-ranging and clear as crystal.

SCOTTISH BAGPIPES: Forthright, distinctive and unmistakable.

SQUARE DANCE FIDDLE: Folksy, down-to-earth, toe-tapping—sprightly and full of energy.

ENCHANTING OBOE: Haunting, charming, disarming—even the cobra is harmless with this sound.

MELLOW CELLO: Deep, sonorous, compassionate—adding body and depth to the orchestra.

PIPE ORGAN: Grand, magnificent, rich—versatile and commanding.

HERALDING TRUMPET: Stirring, lively, invigorating—signaling attention and attack.

CLASSICAL GUITAR: Contemplative, profound, thoughtful *and* thought-provoking.

ONE-MAN BAND: Able to do many things well, all at once.

COMB AND TISSUE PAPER: Makeshift, original, uncomplicated—home-spun and creative.

SWINGING TROMBONE: Warm, rich—great in solo or background support.

INTRODUCTION TO THE ISSUE

LEADER:

- **Summarize these remarks (in your own words) into a brief introduction (no longer than 5 minutes).**
- **Be careful not to read the entire presentation to the group.**
- **In your presentation cover the "Discuss the Issue" questions listed on Side One of the Handout.**

An obscure verse buried in Deuteronomy 24:5 is amazingly practical for married couples:

> If a man has recently married, he must not be sent to war or have any other duty laid on him. For one year he is to be free to stay at home and bring happiness to the wife he has married.

Without benefit of such advice, many couples approach marriage in just the opposite way. They continue to do most of the things they were doing as singles and simultaneously launch into a host of new things as a couple. Consequently, by the end of the first few years, the couple feels overwhelmed by duty and is ready to withdraw to save what happiness can be salvaged.

Jesus observed a rhythm in his life that many couples would do well to learn—the rhythm of retreat and advance. This is the pattern of spirituality practiced by Jesus with his disciples. His first move after his baptism (and prior to beginning his active ministry) was to go to the wilderness (Mark 1:12–13); then he went to the synagogue and to homes in Capernaum (Mark 1:16–34). The night of his first healing ministry was followed by another withdrawal to the wilderness (Mark 1:35). The next day (after healing a man with leprosy), Jesus withdrew again, and "stayed outside in lonely places" (Mark 1:45). Throughout the three years of Jesus' public ministry this rhythm continued: withdrawal followed by advance. Finally, he was in Gethsemane, watching and praying—then he rose to meet the betrayer and fulfilled his greatest service: he died on the cross for the sake of humanity (Mark 14:32–42).

Four Basic Commitments

Withdrawal and waiting doesn't automatically lead to advance and effectiveness, however. A couple's effectiveness in service depends on what they do when they are on their own. Lloyd Ogilvie speaks of "four basic commitments" by which a Christian couple "keeps the drive alive." These principles provide useful guidelines for couples who want to serve the needs of society together.

- **As a couple, make (or renew) an unreserved commitment to Christ.** Talk about Jesus Christ together. Consider the relationships he established, the message of life he presented, the personal sacrifice he went through in order to make this happen, and the summons he presented to his disciples on the basis of his resurrection. Fall in love with Jesus Christ all over again. Let him know you are willing to place him in the very center of your lives.
- **As a couple, commit yourselves to seek an unlimited infilling of the Holy Spirit's power.** Ogilvie puts it so clearly: "As I understand it, our will done in our own strength is humanism. Christ's will done on our own strength is religion. And his will, done by his power, is the abundant life." We are commanded to be filled with the Spirit, to live by the Spirit, and to keep in step with the Spirit.
- **As a couple, commit yourselves to a personal ministry of evangelism.** Don't be thrown off by the word "evangelism." Simply put, it's letting others see and hear Christ through your everyday life and words. It is making known the message of forgiveness and new life in Christ, and seeking to persuade people to respond to that message. Your life in Christ is the result of someone's commitment to this ministry. Now you can be a link in a chain that leads someone else to life in Christ.
- **As a couple, commit yourselves to be involved in at least one of the major crises in your community.** That may include anything from caring for runaway children and the homeless, to bringing practical assistance to those facing poverty and hunger.[15]

Perhaps the process of preparing to serve may be best summed up in a testimony from two friends named Gary and June: "The first couple of years as believers, we were not equipped and we did not know what to do," said Gary, "but a friend showed us some opportunities and helped us prepare to serve. After that, there came a time when we either had to melt back into the crowd or get out there and do it." They are off and running today, investing themselves once a month at a rescue mission, and communicating to the men who come, "We count it a privilege to be with you!"

Serving Together

DISCUSS THE ISSUE (Groups of 4 to 6 / 20 Min.)

1. What is the greatest reason that prevents couples from serving together effectively?
   - ❒ lack of understanding of the needs they could meet
   - ❒ lack of a good model of a couple serving together
   - ❒ lack of time and energy to serve together
   - ❒ lack of training for service
   - ❒ lack of desire to serve anyone other than themselves

2. What prevents you and your spouse from serving together more effectively?

3. Think about marriage partners who are serving together successfully today. From what you can see, how does their partnership work?

RESPOND TO THE BIBLE STUDY (Same Groups / 20 Min.)

***18** After this, Paul left Athens and went to Corinth. [2]There he met a Jew named Aquila,*
a native of Pontus, who had recently come from Italy with his wife Priscilla,
because Claudius had ordered all the Jews to leave Rome. Paul went to see them, [3]and
because he was a tentmaker as they were, he stayed and worked with them. ...
[18]Paul stayed on in Corinth for some time. Then he left the brothers and sailed for Syria,
accompanied by Priscilla and Aquila. ... [19]They arrived at Ephesus, where Paul left Priscilla
and Aquila. ...
[24]Meanwhile a Jew named Apollos, a native of Alexandria, came to Ephesus. He was a
learned man, with a thorough knowledge of the Scriptures. [25]He had been instructed in the
way of the Lord, and he spoke with great fervor and taught about Jesus accurately, though
he knew only the baptism of John. [26]He began to speak boldly in the synagogue. When
Priscilla and Aquila heard him, they invited him to their home and explained to him the way
of God more adequately.

Acts 18:1–3,18a,19a,24–26

1. Which of Priscilla and Aquila's joint projects appeals to you most?
   - ❒ running a business for Jesus' sake
   - ❒ opening a guest house for travelling ministers and others sent from God
   - ❒ going on a short-term mission project
   - ❒ hosting a house church or small group in our home
   - ❒ offering the gift of hospitality to those who need it

2. As a couple, what kind of service do you see yourselves offering one, five or 10 years from now? How could this group help you reach these goals?

INTRODUCTION TO THE BIBLE STUDY

The clearest example in the New Testament of a husband and wife serving together is Priscilla and Aquila. They are an ethnically mixed couple of varied economic background—she from a wealthy Roman family, he once a Jewish slave. We first meet Priscilla and Aquila in Acts 18, when the apostle Paul enters the city of Corinth. Paul looked them up because he needed to earn a living while he was trying to start a church. Since he was a skilled tentmaker and leatherworker, he was able to work at the shop which Aquila and Priscilla owned. The three of them also teamed up in a ministry to get the church started at Ephesus, with spin-off ministries in several other cities as well. Priscilla and Aquila's reputation for starting house churches was well-established and appreciated by Paul, who spoke of them as "my fellow workers in Christ Jesus." He goes on to say: "They risked their lives for me. Not only I but all the churches of the Gentiles are grateful to them" (Rom. 16:3–4).

REFERENCE NOTES

Acts 18:1–3,18a,19a,24–26

18:2 ***Aquila ... Priscilla .*** Priscilla was most likely a Roman citizen of some wealth, while Aquila was born a Jewish slave in the province of Pontus (on the south shore of the Black Sea). How he gained his freedom, went to Rome, and married Priscilla is not revealed. Apparently, Aquila and Priscilla owned tentmaking shops in Rome, Corinth and Ephesus, and traveled between the cities when business or political need dictated. This couple (apparently converted in Rome prior to meeting Paul) became important coworkers with him (v. 26; Rom. 16:3; 1 Cor. 16:19; 2 Tim. 4:19).

18:3 ***tentmaker.*** Paul was a businessman who made tents (either of goat hair or leather) for a living in order to support himself and not to be an economic burden on those he came to serve as a "not-for-profit" preacher (Acts 20:33–34; 1 Thess. 2:9). Paul would have learned tentmaking as a youth, as it was a Jewish custom that all sons were trained in manual work (even if they were rich or aspired to be rabbis). Since rabbis were not paid for their teaching, it was necessary to have a trade.

18:19 ***Ephesus.*** An important center of commerce, culture and religion in the Roman Empire. Ephesus was strategic to Paul's mission vision.

Paul left Priscilla and Aquila. They would scout out the best places and most receptive people with which to start a church.

18:24–26 While Apollos was an earnest, articulate believer in Jesus, he had not received the whole story of the Gospel. Just what he was lacking is unclear, but (as the story in 19:1–7 indicates) he may not have heard of the coming of the Spirit, promised to those who are baptized in the name of Jesus. Both the hospitality and teaching gifts of Priscilla and Aquila are demonstrated in the way they reached out to Apollos and instructed him.

SESSION SEVEN AFFIRMATION AND EVALUATION

Serving Together

ICE-BREAKER / All Together / 15 Minutes (Total)

Musical Instruments. If you had to create an orchestra out of your group, who would you nominate for these instruments? Read over the list and pick an instrument that best describes how you feel about each person in this group. Then ask one person to listen while the others tell this person which instrument they chose for them. Go around the circle so that everyone is affirmed.

ANGELIC HARP: Soft, gentle, melodious, wooing with heavenly sounds.

OLD-FASHIONED WASHBOARD: Nonconforming, childlike and fun.

PLAYER PIANO: Mischievous, raucous, honky-tonk—delightfully carefree.

KETTLE DRUM: Strong, vibrant, commanding when needed but usually in background.

PASSIONATE CASTANET: Full of Spanish fervor—intense and always upbeat.

STRADIVARIUS VIOLIN: Priceless, exquisite, soul-piercing—with the touch of the Master.

FLUTTERING FLUTE: Tender, lighthearted, wide-ranging and clear as crystal.

SCOTTISH BAGPIPES: Forthright, distinctive and unmistakable.

SQUARE DANCE FIDDLE: Folksy, down-to-earth, toe-tapping—sprightly and full of energy.

ENCHANTING OBOE: Haunting, charming, disarming—even the cobra is harmless with this sound.

MELLOW CELLO: Deep, sonorous, compassionate—adding body and depth to the orchestra.

PIPE ORGAN: Grand, magnificent, rich—versatile and commanding.

HERALDING TRUMPET: Stirring, lively, invigorating—signaling attention and attack.

CLASSICAL GUITAR: Contemplative, profound, thoughtful *and* thought-provoking.

ONE-MAN BAND: Able to do many things well, all at once.

COMB AND TISSUE PAPER: Makeshift, original, uncomplicated—homespun and creative.

SWINGING TROMBONE: Warm, rich—great in solo or background support.

EVALUATION / CARING TIME / 30 Minutes

Take a few minutes to review your experience and reflect. Go around on each question and share your answers. When you have finished with the questions, take time to share prayer requests and close in prayer.

1. When you first started this course, how were you feeling?
2. How did you feel about opening up and sharing yourself with this group?
3. What was one of the most significant things you learned?
4. What was the high point in this course for you?
5. What did you appreciate most about the group?

CONTINUATION

Do you want to continue as a group? If so, what do you need to improve? Finish the sentence:

"If I were to suggest one thing we could work on as a group, it would be ... "

MAKE A COVENANT

A covenant is a promise made to each other in the presence of God. Its purpose is to indicate your intention to make yourselves available to one another for the fulfillment of the purposes you share. In a spirit of prayer, work your way through the following sentences, trying to reach an agreement on each statement pertaining to your ongoing life together. Write out your covenant like a contract, stating your purpose, goals, and the ground rules for your group.

1. The purpose of our group will be:

2. Our goals will be:

3. We will meet for _____weeks, after which we will decide if we wish to continue as a group.

4. We will meet from _____ to ______ and we will strive to start on time and end on time.

5. We will meet at ____________________ (place) or we will rotate from house to house.

6. We will agree to the following ground rules for our group (check):

   ❒ PRIORITY: While you are in the course, you give the group meetings priority.

   ❒ PARTICIPATION: Everyone participates and no one dominates.

   ❒ RESPECT: Everyone is given the right to their own opinion, and all questions are encouraged and respected.

   ❒ CONFIDENTIALITY: Anything that is said in the meeting is never repeated outside the meeting.

   ❒ EMPTY CHAIR: The group stays open to new people at every meeting.

- ❐ SUPPORT: Permission is given to call upon each other in time of need at any time.
- ❐ ACCOUNTABILITY: We agree to let the members of the group hold us accountable to the commitments which each of us make in whatever loving ways we decide upon.
- ❐ ADVICE-GIVING: Unsolicited advice is not allowed.
- ❐ MISSION: We agree to do everything in our power to start a new group as our mission.

Other courses in this series of VIDEO COURSES are listed below. For more information about other group resources and possible direction, please contact your small group coordinator or SERENDIPITY at 1-800-525-9563 or visit us at: www.serendipityhouse.com.

DIVORCE RECOVERY: Picking Up the Pieces

HEALTHY RELATIONSHIPS: Living Within Defined Boundaries

PARENTING ADOLESCENTS: Easing the Way to Adulthood

12 STEPS: The Path to Wholeness

DEALING WITH GRIEF & LOSS: Hope In the Midst of Pain

STRESS MANAGEMENT: Finding the Balance

BLENDED FAMILIES: Yours, Mine, Ours

RESOURCES FOR FURTHER STUDY

The *Serendipity Bible for Groups* contains a number of Questionnaire Bible Studies. Generally there is no "right" answer to these questions. The answers reflect your understanding and your experience. The name for this sort of small group exercise is relational Bible Study, since the focus is more on the people in the group than on delving deeply into the text. You can do more rigorous Bible Study by using the questions in the margin of the *Serendipity Bible for Groups*.

There are six courses concerning marriage in the *Serendipity Bible for Groups*. In addition, what follows are 14 suggested studies—seven from the Old Testament and seven from the New Testament. While these questionnaire studies do not always focus directly on marriage, they discuss some aspect of the topic. You will need to adapt the studies so that they focus more closely on the issue. Brief suggestions are given below on how to focus the study. These studies are listed in the order in which they occur in the Bible, not in the order in which you will necessarily want to study them.

Studies From the Old Testament

1. The Fall (Genesis 3:1–24)
   Focus on the issue of conflict and blame-shifting in marriage and how to resolve it effectively.
2. Isaac Born; Ishmael Sent Away (Genesis 21:1–21)
   Focus on how God and your faith helps you deal with conflict in your marriage.
3. Isaac and Rebekah (Genesis 24:1–29,50–67)
   Focus on the history of your marriage relationship and how God is in control.
4. Jacob Marries Leah and Rachel (Genesis 29:1–30).
   Focus on your marriage vows and the priority of putting your marriage first.
5. Ruth Meets Boaz (Ruth 2:1–23)
   Focus on how you can love, honor and cherish your spouse.
6. David Brings the Ark to Jerusalem (2 Samuel 6:1–23)
   Focus on the power of words in your marriage relationship.
7. Viva La Difference! (Song of Songs 6:13–8:4)
   Focus on intimacy and sexuality within the marriage relationship.

Studies From the New Testament

1. An Angel Appears to Joseph (Matthew 1:18–25)
   Focus on your marriage commitment and what you can do to strengthen it.

2. The Parable of the Unmerciful Servant (Matthew 18:21–35)
   Focus on the three hardest words to say in any marriage, "I am sorry."

3. Jesus Heals and Prays (Mark 1:29–39)
   Focus on strengthening your spiritual life together and managing the stress in your lives.

4. Jesus Anointed by a Sinful Woman (Luke 7:36–50)
   Focus on the kind of lovers you are—stingy ones or big ones.

5. At the Home of Martha and Mary (Luke 10:38–42)
   Focus on each other's personality and how to live together in the daily "grind" of life.

6. Jesus Talks With a Samaritan Woman (John 4:7–30)
   Focus on appreciating the differences that exist between you as a couple.

7. Jesus Washes the Disciples' Feet (John 13:1–17)
   Focus on ways of helping and supporting each other in your marriage.

ENDNOTES:

[1]Walter Trobisch, *I Married You* (San Francisco: Harper & Row Publishers, 1971), pp. 12–20.
[2]Ibid., p. 12.
[3]Ibid., p. 18.
[4]Walter Wangerin, Jr., *As For Me and My House* (Nashville: Thomas Nelson, Inc., 1987), p. 31.
[5]Liturgy developed by David Brown. These words are used at the time of the lighting of the unity candle.
[6]Walter Trobisch, *I Married You* (San Francisco: Harper & Row Publishers, 1971), p. 76.
[7]Angela Pintar, *How to Have a Good Fight* (University Counseling Service, University of Wisconsin, Madison, 1984).
[8]George Bach, *The Intimate Enemy*, quoted in Sell, *Achieving the Impossible: Intimate Marriage* (Portland, OR: Multnomah Press, 1982), p. 111.
[9]As mentioned by Richard C. Meyer in an article, "Ideas in Faith for Small Groups" in *Faith at Work* magazine.
[10]Dennis Rainey, *Family Life Conferences: A Weekend to Remember* (Campus Crusade for Christ International, 1987), p. 75.
[11]Miriam Arond and Samuel Pauker, *The First Year of Marriage* (Warner Books, 1987), pp. 256–258.
[12]Billy Graham, *The Marriage Affair*, ed. J. Allan Peterson (Wheaton, IL: Tyndale House, 1981), p. 369.
[13]Miriam Arond and Samuel Pauker, *The First Year of Marriage* (Warner Books, 1987), p. 264.
[14]David Mace, as quoted in H. Norman Wright, *The Pillars of Marriage* (Glendale, CA: Gospel Light Publications, 1979), p. 19.
[15]Lloyd Ogilvie, "Keeping the Drive Alive," *Leadership Journal* (Summer, 1989), p. 19.

PERSONAL
NOTES